2nd Editio

TEARS OF SORROW, SEEDS OF HOPE

A Jewish Spiritual Companion
for Infertility and Pregnancy Loss

RABBI NINA BETH CARDIN

JEWISH LIGHTS Publishing
Woodstock, Vermont

Tears of Sorrow, Seeds of Hope, Second Edition:
A Jewish Spiritual Companion for Infertility and Pregnancy Loss

2007 First Printing, Second Edition
1999 First Edition
© 2007 and 1999 by Nina Beth Cardin

Library of Congress has catalogued the first edition as follows:
Tears of sorrow, seeds of hope : a Jewish spiritual companion for infertility and
    pregnancy loss / [compiled and edited] by Nina Beth Cardin.
        p.   cm.
    Includes bibliographical references.
    ISBN-13: 978-1-58023-017-9
    ISBN-10: 1-58023-017-2
    1. Jewish women—Prayer-books and devotions—English.   2. Judaism—
Prayer-books and devotions—English.   3. Infertility—Religious aspects—
Judaism.   4. Miscarriage—Religious aspects—Judaism.   5.
Children—Death—Religious aspects—Judaism.   I. Cardin, Nina Beth.
BM667.W6T4   1998
296.7'2–dc21   98–48901
                                                                          CIP

Second Edition

ISBN-13: 978-1-58023-233-3
ISBN-10: 1-58023-233-7

10 9 8 7 6 5 4 3 2 1

Manufactured in the United States of America

Cover art: Pomegranate illustration by Joel Moskowitz from
    The Hebrew Blessings series
Cover design: Bronwen Battaglia
Text design: Chelsea Dippel

Published by Jewish Lights Publishing
A Division of LongHill Partners, Inc.
Sunset Farm Offices, Route 4
P.O. Box 237
Woodstock, Vermont 05091
Tel: (802) 457-4000, Fax: (802) 457-4004
www.jewishlights.com

*This book is part of my final journey toward healing
after the losses I suffered almost twenty years ago.
In love and faith, I dedicate it to all the children
who never were, to the ones who stayed all too briefly,
and to the families who will never forget them.*

CONTENTS

PREFACE TO THE SECOND EDITION

Since it was first published in 1999, this book has surprised me in two touching ways:

1. It is given as a gesture of care and soothing by a husband, mother or friend even more than it is purchased by the woman herself; and
2. It offers comfort almost as much in simply being held as in being opened.

At least that is what I have heard from those who write to me and speak to me of the book.

There was the mother who so wanted to ease her daughter's pain, but didn't know how. She found that in giving the book, she could inscribe it with words she could not otherwise bring herself to say.

There are the many rabbis who offer the book as their gesture of care, and as testimony to rituals that now sanctify responses to women's overlooked needs.

There was that one man who stopped me in a parking lot and asked if I would wait a minute; he wanted to show me something. He walked over to his car and opened his trunk, in which was lying a copy of my book. He took it out, gingerly, and held it like a baby. He explained that he and his wife had been trying unsuccessfully for years to have a child, and this book was the first resource that ever offered him comfort in his distress. He carries it around in his car as a talisman of comfort.

And there was the woman who spoke to me, with tears in her eyes, of her husband singing to her from the book when she was in the hospital, straining to deliver her baby.

This book is as much theirs as it is mine. Their stories are now woven into it, even as they weave its words into their lives. The book is somehow different in the hands of every person. That is how it should be.

To acknowledge the changing tone and shape each volume assumes in the possession of different readers, to assist it as it morphs itself to fit the particulars of each owner's story, we have introduced "Reflections" sections throughout the book. Each section offers a series of guided journaling questions to help you work through your grief. In this new edition we've also introduced blank pages on which you can record, discover, and otherwise unfold your thoughts, responses, prayers, and wishes.

May this book mold itself to your own needs and may it help carry you to the place you find peace.

ACKNOWLEDGMENTS

No book is the product of one person alone, and this book even more than others benefits from many people's contributions:

I am grateful to Rabbi Michelle Goldsmith, my able and dedicated research assistant, for the time, sensitivity, and effort she invested in the early stages of this book. Rabbi Goldsmith undertook this project as a labor of love when she was a rabbinical student with a schedule and commitments already as full as they could possibly be. Without her dedication, this book would not be as full and as rich as it is.

I had wanted to write this book for over ten years, but it was only when I became the associate director of the National Center for Jewish Healing that the various threads of my life came together to fashion for me the opportunity. I thank the NCJH for giving me the structure, time, and encouragement that enabled me to get started.

The framing of this book has been immeasurably enhanced by my many conversations with Dr. Lois Dubin, who gave graciously of her time, wisdom, and experience. A version of her ritual response to loss may be found in chapter 4 of this book.

Over the course of years, I met and spoke with many families and individuals, acquaintances and strangers, both formally and informally, who shared with me their most intimate experiences of fear, pain, loss, and longing. Their honesty and generosity of spirit are reflected in every page of this book.

I will ever be grateful to Jewish Lights' publisher and president, Stuart M. Matlins, for so readily and heartily agreeing to make this book one of his own and for providing me with a sensitive, knowledgeable, no-nonsense editor, Elisheva Urbas, who was able to help me cut my way through many ideological and structural thickets.

To my husband, who tenderly cared for me as I lost two of the children we had wanted so badly, and who held me as I brought our live children into this world, thank you. You are my strength. And to our children, who fill our home with noise and meaning, you are our joy. To you, I offer the prayer of the psalmist: "May you live to see your children's children; and may there be peace for all Israel." (Ps. 128:6)

NINA BETH CARDIN

INTRODUCTION

My second miscarriage occurred in the fourth month—a missed abortion, the doctor said. The pregnancy should have ended much earlier, but my body held onto the baby as if it were alive. So did my heart, and so did my dreams. Two miscarriages in three pregnancies. That was not what I expected. My friends wondered how could I go on. I wondered how could I give up. But I needed to find solace and strength in my sorrow. The rabbis I turned to were bereft of sources, unable to help me. Still, I needed to hear the soothing voice of my people, to be guided by my grandmothers' ways in mourning and healing. Surely they had wisdom to share with me. But their voices were long lost, and I and so many others were the poorer for it.

It was out of that experience, out of the desire to uncover the hidden ways of women's traditions in loss and infertility, that I decided to write this book.

This is a book for families who have suffered the pains of infertility and pregnancy loss. There are oh so many of us. A fifth to a quarter of all first-time pregnancies yield to loss instead of life. Tens of thousands more women cannot begin or hold a pregnancy without medical intervention. Many of us—young and American—grew up believing that our health and the ability to control what happens to our bodies are our birthright. We are often shocked and humbled by our first encounters with the limitations of the flesh. And many of these first encounters occur in the realm of fertility.

For some of us, becoming a parent is a dream we cherish from childhood. A friend tells the story of a young daughter raised in a house free from the narrow straits of gender-specific toys and the limited roles they may confine her to. Yet one day, the mother walked by the daughter's room—the daughter was all of four or five at the time—and heard what sounded like a lullaby. Peeking in, the mother saw the daughter cradling a huge fire truck in her arms, rocking it back and forth, singing softly to it all the while. When we have the impulse toward parenthood, and most of us do at some point in our lives, it cannot be squelched. We may choose dogs or cats, or plants and flowers, or projects or art to be our "babies." But this impulse always seeks some form of expression, and eventually resolves itself into wanting a child.

Some of us feel this desire early. Others may come to it later in life. We may be encouraged by our spouse, our age, our station, or our private calendar of life. But when we do seek a child, it becomes our passion. And sometimes, we find that though we are ready, it does not happen. We do not become pregnant; we do not hold a pregnancy. All we do is hurt.

Many of us choose to bear this sorrow alone. Perhaps because we do not trust our neighbors and community with our most tender feelings. Perhaps because we fear political misuse of our mourning over a child that is not yet a child. Perhaps because we fear what will happen if we dare to open the gates of our bulging reservoir of pain.

These feelings of emptiness and loss are our most constant companions. They go with us wherever we go; color the air around us; sit beside us at our work, in meetings, at concerts. When they threaten to break out, we try to lock them up. We let them out, if ever, only in the safety of our homes or with our dearest friends. We hide the pregnancies that end too soon and conceal our attempts at conception that fail. Our world contracts, falling into a tangle of numbers: dates, times, counts, measurements.

Yet, even within this private world, many of us would welcome company, a community of comforters we can turn to that knows what we know, has felt what we feel. For despite our different stories, we are joined in a kinship of longing. This book is a product of that kinship. It was created as an act of healing by those of us who suffered once, twice, or more, for those of you who suffer still. It seeks to be a companion, a constant presence, as you walk this path of parenthood.

This is a book of rituals, prayers, and poems written by those who know the loss that has no face, no name, and no grave. We know what it's like to feel life and hope slip away, to be carrying a body where a baby should be. We know what it's like to pass every day that room that still has no crib, to know in our hearts that we were once mothers, even if our only child died in our womb. We know how lonely it is when, weeks after the loss, we have not finished telling our story, but our friends and loved ones—as caring as they may be—have finished listening.

We know the search for reasons and remedies that follows: the doctors, the procedures, the time, the cost, the hopes, the hurt. We do not have the answers. We cannot say to you, "This is the way." But we can offer responses drawn from deep within the wellspring of Judaism and our hearts. And we can tell you that behind these responses are sojourners, men and women like your-self, who are reaching out to you.

"A woman who lost her child came to her teacher for comfort. She poured out her grief as he listened patiently. Then he said to her: 'My child, I cannot wipe away your tears. But I can show you how to make them holy.'"

Many of us who fashioned the words found in this book first sought advice from our rabbis and teachers. We were told, with varying degrees of compassion: Judaism has no ritual for you. It has no way to help you mourn your pain.

But we were not satisfied, and we did not believe it was true. We were not the first generation of Jews to suffer this way. How could it be, then, that we would be the first to respond? We live in an era of great rediscoveries of the mystical, moral, and pietistic ways of Judaism. Surely there is something there for us.

So, we began at the beginning, by rereading the stories of our matriarchs, Sarah, Rebecca, Leah, and Rachel, the ones who could not conceive, carried in pain, but eventually bore the children who brought forth a great nation. We reread the story of Hannah, whose petition for a child became the very emblem of rabbinic prayer and whose son, Samuel, would anoint the first king of Israel. These women cried bitterly over their infertility, blaming themselves, their husbands, their luck. And today we call them mothers.

We found other hints of compassion in later verses: "If you abide by these laws, you shall be blessed from among all the peoples, for there will not be among you a barren man or a barren woman." (Deut. 7:14) And "No one will miscarry or be barren in your land." (Exod. 23:26) Looking past the biblical idea of merit and reward, which may distract and even disturb some of us, we can peer into the very heart of the message: Children are the first of all God's blessings, the first of all gifts the Jews were to enjoy when they entered the Promised Land. Fertility is neither casual nor precisely causal. It is a mystery, a blessing, and it takes the very hand of God to make it happen. The psalmist, too, proclaims fertility as one of life's highest joys and one of the achievements that earn God our eternal praise: "God sets the once-barren woman in her home, now a joyous mother of children. Hallelujah, praised be God." (Ps. 113: 9) In Pirkei Avot we read the following: "Ten miracles occurred at the Temple in Jerusalem when the Jewish people gathered to celebrate. The first one is: no woman ever miscarried from the smell of the sacrifices. . . ."

The more we looked the more we found, and soon an air of comfort and belonging began to settle around us. Our needs had been acknowledged by our tradition. We were not alone, we were not abandoned, we were not marginal. We looked until we were content, or until we ceased to find—either through exhaustion or lack of skill. But we knew we had not found it all. Then we gathered all we had, sat at the water's edge, and began to invent, each in our own time, each in our own way. Here, at least, was a place we could own, a space we could shape. When our world was spinning out of our control, here was something we could grab onto. The doctors would be the guides to our physical healing. The treasures from our tradition would be the guides to our spiritual healing.

Healing came from seeking, finding, belonging, and sharing the fruits of our work with friends in need. It is so very hard to heal alone. The rabbis tell us we can learn the ways of healing from the story of Sarah, wife of Abraham. On one of their sojourns south, Sarah was forced into the harem of Avimelekh, king of Gerar. To protect her, and to warn Avimelekh that something was amiss, God "closed up all the wombs of the house of Avimelekh." (Gen. 20:18) When Avimelekh realized that Sarah was Abraham's wife and therefore not available to him, he released her. Abraham was moved to pray on behalf of the royal household, asking God to restore their fertility. Immediately after that, Sarah, too, conceived. Pain is a demanding master, closing us off to others around us, consuming our attention. But there are times when the veil lifts, and we are able to cast our gaze beyond ourselves and use our pain to bring relief to others. Such moments offer us, too, a taste of healing, if not a cure.

Over the past two decades, a multitude of popular works have appeared discussing the various processes—physiological and emotional—that accompany infertility and pregnancy loss. Such books help their readers better understand what they are experiencing. They explain new therapeutic opportunities and medical resources that are available. They tell of support groups devoted to their readers' particular medical and practical concerns. They help by offering stories of loss, allowing readers to find themselves and lose themselves in the experiences of others. Most good, full-service bookstores have shelves devoted to books on infertility and pregnancy loss.

This book does not seek to duplicate these fine works. Rather, it begins where the others leave off. While the doctors do what they must do, when it is time for us to wait, or hope, or cry, or sleep, or pray, it is time for this book. The passages within it are drawn from the rich pool of spiritual responses that Judaism possesses. They reach out to us and embolden us to join our voices to the ancient prayers designed to get us through the night.

Included here are responses to different kinds of loss—from early spontaneous abortions to neonatal death to the moment it is time to say *enough*. This format of prayers, organized by type of loss or experience, is designed to help you quickly find a response most appropriate to your need. It is quite likely that there may be more than one prayer or ritual that is right for you found in different places throughout the book. Many of us who suffer one kind of loss also suffer another related loss. Miscarriages may give way to difficulty conceiving. Conceiving through medical assistance may yield a miscarriage. So, although the book presents rituals and prayers arranged according to episode, in reality, the prayers you seek may straddle these categories.

In any one section, you will find several prayers and rituals that speak to the same event. A variety of styles validates a variety of voices and, hopefully, encourages each reader to explore her own. Some of us who find ourselves in the position of needing to speak the same desire many times may appreciate the opportunity to use a variety of images and expressions. On the other hand, some of us find comfort in repeating the same prayers again and again. But even we may need to try out several styles before settling on the one that feels best.

All of this points to one of the most important messages of the book: we each mourn differently. We experience anger, shame, blame, confusion, frustration, jealousy, despair, sadness, awe, loss, guilt, and hope in differing amounts. There is no one right way to feel, no one right way to mourn. You are your own expert on creating your path to healing.

Yet, despite the variety, this book is of one piece. It is a place where our stories merge with the stories of our past. We become one with Sarah and Isaac and Rachel and Hannah; we sit in their circle and speak of them by name. The images of the Temple lost and rebuilt, of the moon waxing and waning, become images of our bodies. We learn from the prophets, from Eve and Deborah. Their sadness echoes our sadness, their success gives us hope. We no longer have to bear our pain alone.

These texts, then, are not so much Torah as haggadah, a form of narrative that becomes a model, a structure upon which you can build your own prayers, rituals, and stories. You can—and should—embellish the texts as much as you wish. It is part of the process of renewal. The creators of these works found comfort not only in saying or doing them. We found equal comfort in researching and creating them. For the texts embody the legacy of our ancestors. They form the lap that cradles us as we weep. For many of us, though we began our search by holding the sacred books in our hands, we ended it by feeling that we, in truth, were being held by them.

There are several forms of text in this book. There are *meditations* and *poems*, both ancient and modern, speaking the age-old feelings of loss, longing, and hope. There are *prayers*—words of desire spoken to or about God. And there are *rituals*—deliberate and defined actions performed at designated times either in a group or alone, and often accompanied by symbolic objects and prayer.

Most of us are comfortable with poems. Many of us are fluent in prayer. But few of us think we are ready for rituals. Nothing could be further from the truth. Rituals pervade our lives. Some are self-made, like the way we brush our teeth in the morning or straighten our desk before going home each night. Some are taught, like dressing to go to the theater or celebrating birthdays with a cake. Some are strictly of personal significance, like how our family greets us when we return home every evening; and some are of worldly significance, like how we greet a foreign ruler who comes on a state visit. Yet all are vital. Rituals support our world, fashion our environment, reinforce our values, and help give form and meaning to what would otherwise be a life of chaos.

Rituals speak to us beyond the power of words, through our muscles and skin and breath. They speak in a language that transcends the present. Through them, we become more than we are and more fully what we are. When a Jewish bride puts a veil over her face, she becomes every Jewish woman who has ever loved a man. All love collapses into her love. She is filled with the ways Jewish women have ever loved Jewish men.

Rituals seek change, not of God, but of us. They are designed to move the participants from one state of being or awareness to another. The participants expect, and hope, to be different after a successful ritual than they were before. Whatever its precise task—be it closure, celebration, release, hope, acceptance, or new legal status—the ritual's fundamental purpose is to escort the participants across a threshold, from where they are to where they need to go.

We know the power of ritual from elsewhere in our lives. When we enter a theater, we become an audience. We know the rules: where to sit, how to behave. We know the boundaries. All this prepares us for what will follow. The theater will darken, and, knowing and trusting the power of theater, we will let our world fall away. That's the way it is with rituals. We give ourselves over to them and they in turn transform us, transport us. They work through our bodies, bypassing the radar of our restless, worrisome, skeptical minds, and open us to places and feelings we might have been closed to before. When Abraham Joshua Heschel spoke of marching for civil rights in Selma, Alabama, arm-in-arm with the Reverend Martin Luther King, Jr., he said, "I felt my feet were praying." Through ritual, our bodies pray.

Some of the rituals in this book assume the presence of a gathering of friends and family. But many are just as likely to be conducted by the woman or couple alone. Private rituals may be more comfortable, lessening the sense of self-consciousness and inhibition. Collective rituals, on the other hand, offer an immediate sense of community. Almost every ritual in this book can be conducted either way.

Two valuable components of successful rituals cannot be replicated on paper but cannot be ignored: scents and songs. Both of these help transform the everyday into a sacred space, and a gathering of individuals into a holy union of people. Lighting scented candles may help establish the mood even before the ritual begins. And as one celebrant said: "I believe better and more thoroughly when I'm singing." Seek advice from your rabbi or friends about songs that may be appropriate for you. A *niggun*, a wordless song, is an inviting way to welcome your co-celebrants. It eases tensions and helps unite the mood and intentions of everyone present. It eliminates the barriers of insiders and outsiders, for everyone can participate. And it opens up the soul, preparing it to receive the blessings of the ritual.

Using this book

Because books demand linear organization, the texts presented here have page breaks and chapter divisions, all laid out end to end to end. By its nature, this structure suggests to the reader, "You fit either in this category or that one." Or, "First read this, then read that." And, when the chapter ends, "This is all we have to say about that." But in truth, that is not the case, neither for what we believe nor for what you experience. The structure represents nothing more than the neat and necessary limits of print, not the messy, expansive expressions of our hearts. Emotions follow different rules, rising and falling like the heavings of a mournful chest. Feelings of despair and hope cycle back one on the other, violating any logical sense of progress, spilling into each other, innocent of each other's boundaries. Episodes passed are often revisited. Time transforms itself into a loop. This book seeks to transcend the hegemony of print as much as possible and bend itself to the circuits of the emotions.

You, our reader, are encouraged to read past the spaces. See how the texts from one section blend with those from another. Imagine taking a prayer, a ritual, or a snippet of a psalm from one section and joining it with fragments found elsewhere in the book. The texts you find here are swatches of a cloth woven from the emotions of people's lives. Take from them, and fashion out of them your own garment of comfort.

Sometimes the message of healing can be found not only in prayers and rituals, but in the existence of a book that binds them together. Any book, but especially a prayer book, is a token of a commitment, a banner, a belief. Much more than a photocopy of an article from a magazine somewhere, the presence of a book of prayers on infertility—classical and modern—tells us that those of us who suffer this way have not been abandoned by our people. It tells us that experiences centered within a woman's body are properly the concern of the entire Jewish people. No more can rabbis say: Judaism has no ritual for you.

Such liturgical confirmation will not cure our condition or replace our loss. But sometimes simply holding a book made by our people, cast from our tradition, and carrying our dreams can help us as we struggle toward the light.

Reflections and Journaling

In this second edition, we made a place for your voice. In shaded portions throughout the book, and in blank pages at the back, we invite you to add your stories, memories, and insights to the growing legacy of Jewish infertility traditions. Tradition is built that way. Not all in one swoop; not only by the authorities. But by what we, the people, do in our homes and communities, by how we respond and who we tell.

Healing perhaps best reveals itself in stories—the telling, retelling, and retelling yet again of our experiences. As we speak the story, and craft the story, we mold it. We give it shape and handles and boundaries, so that it no longer threatens to swallow us up. Rather, we have a hand-hold with which to grab our grief and guide it. Loss and pain are like a wild horse upon which we are riding. We are tossed and bruised and carried along for the ride. But through speaking the story and writing it down, with the pen as our reins, we can tame its bucking and bouncing, even if we do not know where it, or we, are ultimately going.

May this book prove to be a faithful companion to all who pursue their journey toward parenthood.

A word to friends and family who are buying this book for loved ones

Giving this book to loved ones is a tender expression of your caring, a symbol of your desire to be present in their time of need. That gesture alone can help them as they build their reservoir of comfort. However, your loved ones may respond differently to the contents of the book than you might hope or expect. They might use different prayers than you might have selected. Or they may cherish the gift, and what it represents, but still put it aside for now. It may be too early for them to turn to the words and rituals they find in here. It may be that God and prayer are not active players in their lives. It may be that they are turning to other ways of healing. As long as those ways are not destructive, that is okay, and your gift is still a welcome gift. But you must let your loved ones decide what is best for them. Your task is to be with them as they work through their ways of mourning, of gaining strength, sustaining hope, and moving on when decisions must be made. Too often in our pain for them, in our need to help them and comfort ourselves, we hold a vision of what our loved ones should do. It is appropriate to share these thoughts with them, but then we must step back and let them decide.

Most often in these matters, each heart is its own best counsel.

1

In the Beginning

Love poems

For some, the first glimpse of infertility begins in the disappointing recurrence of the familiar. Our period returns, our breasts do not get tender, everything is the same when it ought to be so different. The door of fear eases itself open. Is there something wrong? Quickly, we seek to shut it, reassuring ourselves: "Sometimes these things take time." "Wait until next month." "Too much stress at the office." "We just have to relax." And in most cases, this is true. These past months were probably nothing more than missed timing, bad luck, or a system long out of use preparing itself for business.

But in that moment of uncertainty, in that need to reassure ourselves, we become vulnerable. Fear begins to dampen our hope and tension begins to slide in between us and our partner. We know it is much too soon for us to feel betrayed by our bodies; too

soon for our bed, our haven of pleasure and comfort, to be trans-
formed into a place of work. *Too soon,* we tell ourselves. And yet
the worries begin: Is it me? Is it him? Is it us together? Am I being
punished because of that time when . . .

These thoughts come unwelcome, unbidden. They crowd
the bed and dull the passions. Easy, joyous intimacy is an early
victim. But the tension can be held at bay, exiled for at least a
moment, by the age-old potion of love poems. Looking at the one
we love and speaking the intimate words of man and woman can
carry us off to faraway places and open us up to desire and hope
once again.

You may have your favorite love poems or your favorite
songs that speak of your tenderness, awe, joy, and passion. Now is
a good time to reach for them.

Or you can claim the erotic words of the Bible's Song of
Songs that lovers have whispered to each other for thousands of
years. You might choose to read select verses or whole sections.
The book is only eight short chapters. Some English versions present the text as dialogue, allowing you to follow what she says and
he says. Seek out several translations and choose the one that suits
you best. Here is a sampling to get you started:

Song of Songs

He: Kiss me with the kisses of your mouth, for your love is
sweeter than wine. The scent of your oils is lovely, your
name is like the finest fragrance spread over me. (1:2–3)

She: I am a rose of Sharon, a lily of the valley. Draw me
after you, let us run . . . let us delight and rejoice in our
love. (1:4)

He: You are fair, my darling, you are fair, your eyes are like a
dove's; your lips a crimson thread, your mouth so come-
ly. (4:3) Your body is long like a palm tree, your breasts

clusters of grapes. I say, I will climb this palm tree, and grasp onto its branches. Let your breasts be as clusters of grapes, and the scent of your breath like apples in bloom. (7:8–9)

She: And you, my beloved, are handsome, beautiful indeed. Your cheeks are like boughs of spices, mounds of sweet herbs; your lips are like lilies, shimmering with flowing myrrh. This is my beloved and this is my friend, daughters of Jerusalem. (5:13, 16)

He: Our couch is in a bower; cedars are the beams of our house, cypresses the rafters. (1:15–16)

She: He brought me to the banquet room and his banner of love was over me. . . . His left hand was under my head, his right arm embraced me. I adjure you, maidens of Jerusalem, by gazelles or by hinds of the field, do not wake or rouse love until it please. (2:4–7; 3:5)

He: My dove, in the cranny of the rocks, hidden by the cliff, let me see your face, let me hear your voice, for your voice is sweet and your face is pure beauty. (2:14) You have captured my heart, my own, my bride, with one glance of your eyes, with one strand of your necklace. How sweet is your love, my own, my bride. (4:9–10)

She: Let us go early to the vineyards; let us see if the vine has flowered; if its blossoms have opened, if the pomegranates are in bloom. There I will give my love to you. (7:13)

Found in no fewer than fourteen books of the Bible, the pomegranate is deeply embedded in the culture of the Jewish people, evoking images of love, fertility, beauty, piety, learning, sensuality, and feminine sexuality. The Israelite spies brought pomegranates to the Jewish people gathered at the borders of Israel as proof of the fecundity of the land they were destined to inherit. The passionate poet in the Song of Songs sings of his lover's cheeks as slices of pomegranate and her "groove as a pomegranate grove." (Song of Songs 4:13) The hem of the robe of the High Priest was adorned with a row of pomegranates *(cont. on next page)*

Reflections

When distractions or fears seem to crowd the bed, write or recite a love poem to one another. Speak of the joy you find in each other's presence, in the warmth and comfort of each other's body. Feel how deep, enveloping, and fulfilling it is to lie with each other. Stir the passions, appreciate the pleasure. Those too are God's gifts.

Transcribe or write a favorite love poem in your journal or in the pages at the back of this book. Or attach a card, letter, or note that one of you wrote to the other in the early days of your romance. Turn to it, and add to it, whenever you desire.

Prayers of hope

The Midrash—an imaginative exploration into the words, images, and stories of the Torah—tells us that it takes three to make a

---

(cont. from previous page) and gilded bells, as prescribed by the Torah: ". . . and upon the skirts of the robe you shall make pomegranates of blue and purple and scarlet, with bells of gold between them round about: a golden bell and a pomegranate; a golden bell and a pomegranate." (Exod. 28:33–34) The pillars of the Temple were likewise generously draped in ribbons of pomegranates. A thumb-shaped, ivory pomegranate from the ninth century B.C.E. is the only known relic of the Temple of Solomon. The words "Sacred donation for the priests of the house of YHVH" are inscribed upon it.

The rabbis, hundreds of years later, saw the pomegranate as a symbol of the Jew, with the seeds representative of the good deeds that reside in each of us, or as the house of study, with the seeds representative of the schoolchildren arrayed in their seats. *Ketubot*, Jewish marriage contracts, were often adorned with drawings of pomegranates. A pomegranate charm may be worn as a fertility amulet or simply as a symbol that a couple awaits God's blessing.

child: a man, a woman, and God. That is to say, conception is a mystery begun by lovers but nurtured and countenanced by God. In eighteenth-century Italy, Jewish women seeking to become pregnant would speak of the mystery, recall the divine kindness shown to our barren foremothers, and beseech God to remember them, and all barren women, with kindness as well:

To be said on the evening the couple wishes to conceive

My God and God of my mothers and fathers, may it be Your will that You be gracious to us tonight. Make tonight a night of peace and joy, tenderness and loving, a night on which my beloved and I conceive a child. Hold us close in Your embrace, God, just as we hold each other tightly. Remember us as You remembered Sarah. Care for us as You cared for Rebecca. Tend to us as You tended to our mothers, Leah and Rachel.

Choose from Your sacred treasury of souls, and give us a child who is wise and caring, healthy and secure. May we be blessed with a pregnancy that lasts, with a birth that yields life, and a child who gives us joy.

May our family grow through the years, and through Your kindness, may we be a blessing to all who know us.

May the words of our mouths and the desires of our hearts please You, our Strength and our Deliverer.

Sarah was the first mother of the Jewish people. Joining her husband, Abraham, she answered God's call to go out from her ancestral home and journey to the Promised Land to found a new nation. Despite all expectations of blessings, she bore no children. "God has closed me up, stopped me from bearing children" (Gen. 16:2), she told Abraham. She was ninety when God appeared to Abraham, as Sarah stood by the entrance to the tent. God said to Abraham: "At this time next year, Sarah will have a son." (Gen. 18:14) Sarah laughed when she heard this, as did Abraham, for they did not believe that two people as old as they could now bring forth a child. But "God remembered Sarah" (Gen. 21:1), and a year later, she bore a son and called him Isaac, meaning "he shall laugh."

Rebecca was our second matriarch, Sarah's daughter-in-law, Isaac's wife. She, too, was unable to conceive. "And Isaac prayed for her, for she was barren, and God answered his prayers, and she became pregnant."(Gen. 25:21) But Rebecca had great pain in her pregnancy, so great that she was moved to approach God to ask why she suffered so. And God told her: "You are carrying twins, each the father of a great nation. And though you suffer, you will safely give birth to two healthy boys." (Gen. 25:23) Both Rachel and Leah, Jacob's wives, also suffered bouts of infertility and sought help from God, their husband, and remedies plucked from the field.

Infertility is a part of our founding story. It is written in holy letters in our holiest of books, black fire on a river of light. Why? Perhaps to teach us that our biblical mothers were not merely the accidental wives of their husbands, Mrs. Abraham, Mrs. Isaac, and Mmes. Jacob, not incubators for their husbands' seed, but leaders chosen for greatness by God. How could God show us—even more, show our mothers, who were so unused to being valued on their own—that they were not mere instruments of their husbands' divine destiny? Through the part of women that men could touch but not own, could desire but not control: the womb. And so, for our mothers, the activity of the womb became a sign of God's election.

A prayer for the woman when she lies with her husband

You spread Your light over me like a robe
smoothing the heaven of its wrinkles and folds.
You built the vaulted sky with beams of water
and set Your chariot high upon the clouds
to ride on the wings of the wind.
You water the mountains from the chambers on high
and satisfy the needs of the earth with the fruit of Your labor.

How plentiful are Your works, God.
Everything You do in wisdom.
The earth is full of Your blessings.
Let me be filled with them too.

Reflections

Some people love writing. For them, the white spaces of the pages at the back of this book are welcome invitations to join forces with the voices within this work, to pick up where they leave off. Other people are uncomfortable writing or journaling. No matter who you are, we want to encourage you to think of these spaces as your spaces. They are meant to help make this book your book, to help you chronicle your emotions and experiences along the path toward parenting.

If you are a writer, write away. Talk about your feelings, your hopes, your fears. If you are not a writer, make lists. We can all be list-makers.

Make a list of the words and feelings that are swirling in your head—those that brought you to this book or surround your reading of this book.

Here are suggestions for both writer and list-maker:

I came to own this book because ...

Right before I sat down here I was ...

I opened this book now because ...

Right now I am ...

From where I am sitting I can see ...

When I put this book down I will ...

The things I hope for include ...

Mikveh prayers: a cool, private place

The *mikveh* is a body of clear water found in the pools of nature or created by gathering rain in a specially built cistern. The water must be deep enough so that a person, when immersed, will be completely covered from head to toe. For 3,000 years Jewish women have visited the *mikveh* monthly in a rite of sexual, spiritual, and procreative renewal. Today, women are reclaiming this ancient tradition, on both a monthly and occasional basis, in search of hope and healing. The name *mikveh* itself is a promise of comfort, for it echoes of the word *tikvah*, meaning expectation and hope.

Even more, *Mikveh Yisrael* is a name that refers to God. "God is *Mikveh Yisrael;* all who leave You will despair, for they have forsaken the source of the living waters. Heal me, God, and I will be healed. Save me and I will be saved." (Jer. 17:13–14) Jeremiah, a prophet tortured by his calling and the suffering of the Jews, held fast to God, proclaiming that the waters of God's mercy are filled with life. They wash over us, soothe us, and remove our despair

When we enter the *mikveh*, then, we enter a realm of the divine, for the waters of the *mikveh* are drawn from the heavens, a fountain of blessings rained down from the skies. The waters of the *mikveh* conjure up memories of the waters of Creation, which, at God's word, separated and gave birth to the universe of life. In our hour of need, we enter these waters, a gift of heaven held close by earth. We ask the waters to part, close up around us, hold us, and then give birth to a woman who will give birth to a child. We stand naked in the water, take a breath, and go under. For a moment we feel the waters hold us, strong and gentle. And then we emerge, fresh and new, our bodies sequined with droplets of hope.

At the *mikveh*, the woman enters a private dressing room where she bathes thoroughly, preparing herself physically and spiritually to enter the ritual bath. For women suffering loss or infertility, this is a particularly tender moment, for we are called upon to tend to the body we fear may be failing us. This becomes a time of awareness and reconciliation, of making peace with our bodies. It is a time of acknowledgment of all the good places our bodies have taken us and a time of hope for all our bodies may yet do this month.

Some women who enter the *mikveh* choose to recite a *kavvanah*, a personal, often self-composed meditation that speaks of deep intentionality in the most down-to-earth way. It generally begins: Here I am, prepared and ready to perform this mitzvah of . . . May this act serve to . . . Or: Through this act may I. . . .

The following prayer, based on the blessing said when announcing the new moon, can be said in addition to or instead of your personal *kavvanah*:

A prayer for a child— to be said before entering the *mikveh*

El Malei Rachamim, God full of mercy, with an overflowing heart I approach the waters of the *mikveh*, gathered from the rain sent here from the heavens. Let these waters rush strong against my body, washing away all sadness and sorrow, all worries and fears. Let them refresh my soul and restore my strength.

God, as my cycle begins anew, let these coming weeks be a time of rejoicing; let this month be the season our dreams come true. Let our house be filled with promise and joy, with the rays of Your radiance shining upon us. It is to You we turn, God; in You we trust.

Barukh ata adonai eloheinu melekh ha'olam, asher kiddeshanu b'mitzvotav v'tzivanu al hatevilah.

Blessed are You, God of all creation, who sanctifies us through Your commandments and commands us regarding immersion.

A prayer for the woman to say as she is dressing to return home

To my lover
I weave a hymn of love and joy to you
to be one with you is all that I desire,
to be sheltered in the shadow of your hand
to know the hidden mystery of your fire.

So, God, drape me in the fragrant sheets of heaven.
Bind my clothes with cords of satin, soft as a dove.

There are many names for God in the Jewish tradition: *Mikveh Yisrael; HaMakom,* The Place; *Avinu Malkeinu,* Our Father and King; *Ribono Shel Olam,* Master of the Universe; and many more. The one that finds favor here is *El Malei Rachamim.* This may sound discordant to the traditional ear, for *El Malei Rachamim* is the name of choice in the classic prayer of loss, mourning, and remembrance.

But the imagery evoked by these words is too rich to limit to death. The word *rachamim,* meaning mercy, is associated with the word *rechem,* meaning womb. *Malei* means full, specifically here, full in the womb, the way we wish to be. *El* is God. These are the divine images we seek: a God knowing intimately of our desires, bulging at the belly with kindness for us, standing at the boundary of the place from which all life flows and to which all life returns.

Another name that can be found in some of these prayers is *El Shaddai,* a term of unknown origin. Some believe it may come from Akkadian, meaning mountain. Others believe it may mean one who feeds and nurtures. But whatever its etymology, *Shaddai* is a homophone of the Hebrew word meaning "breasts," and it conjures up a God who holds us close, feeds us, comforts us, and listens for our cry when we are in need.

Braid my hair as you did Eve's once in Eden.
And send your angels to guide me safely to my love.

Reflections

The *mikveh* may be a comforting, familiar place to you. Or it may be a strange, exotic (even a bit frightening?) experience. Or perhaps something in between. Whichever it is, try recording the moment.

> *At the mikveh I was feeling ...*
>
> *In the mikveh I thought about ...*
>
> *On the way home I talked / thought about ...*
>
> *The things I like about my body include ...*
>
> *If asked how I feel about my body,*
> *I would say ...*

If you cannot go to a *mikveh*, you may want to create a water experience in your own bath. Choose the most comforting tub you can find and fill it with water. Bubbles, bath beads, scented oils, and perfumed candles can all enhance the moment. Favorite calming music can set the mood.

Lower yourself into the water. Feel at ease with your body; inhabit it, cheer it, soothe it, possess it. And come out renewed and refreshed.

2

Give Me a Child: Prayers for Conception

Infertility is a subtle adversary. It does not ambush us on the road or burst in upon us unawares. Instead, it slowly, steadily reveals itself. Month after month, period after period, pregnancy after pregnancy, it discloses a bit more of its awful face. Each time, we try to look away, to pretend it is not there.

But one day, after one period too many, after one loss too many, we are forced to see it. And then we feel it all around us, claiming us, clawing us, defining who we are. Infertility becomes the measure of our lives. We no longer count time by days on the calendar but by the cycles of our flow, the periods we have come to hate, and the anniversary of our miscarriages.

It wasn't supposed to be this way. Most modern women spend their earliest years of sexual awareness trying *not* to get pregnant. The unspoken expectation is that without protection, pregnancy happens. As gaining weight is to eating, so pregnancy is to unprotected sex—so we thought when we were younger. If we had been looking for any prayers about pregnancy back then, they would have been, "Oh please, God, tell me I'm just late." And so, we thought, it would continue to be throughout our "childbearing years." Only it isn't. Not for us. Not now. So we begin the hard work of reversing expectations and overcoming the shock, the worries, the guilt, the blame, the shame, the fears.

For some of us, becoming pregnant is not the problem. Holding the pregnancy is. We become pregnant, just as we anticipated, only to find that it ends too soon.

Still others among us may have known all along that we are not able to conceive. When we were younger, this knowledge slumbered, barely noticed in the landscape of a busy, fully-forming self. Now, however, it prowls our days.

Reflections

Each of us sees a different face of infertility. But there is a strong family resemblance that allows us, encourages us, to be present to the needs of each other. It is fascinating that infertility is written into the sacred story of the Jewish people. As invisible as it is today, infertility is writ large in our shared memory. We begin with four mothers: Sarah, Rebecca, Leah, and Rachel. Each struggled, in differing ways, to bear children. Sarah could not conceive; Rebecca went into premature labor and feared she would lose the pregnancy; Leah had secondary infertility—the inability to conceive after previously giving birth; Rachel had primary infertility. Then there is

Hannah, the woman who gave birth to the prophet who coronated Israel's first king and laid the groundwork for Israel's national identity. She also struggled to conceive.

But tradition tells us that these women did not suffer their pain alone. God attended to each of them. God approached Sarah, telling her she would overcome her infertility. Rebecca approached God, seeking answers from God about why she suffered. And God responded. Leah and Rachel, under divine tutelage, negotiated means for resolving their infertility. Hannah devoted her annual pilgrimage to beseeching God to give her a child.

Not with regard to any other aspect of their lives do we see these women—or almost any other woman in the Torah—approaching God. Not about love or marriage, rain or food, farming or spinning, or even sickness. These women are shown approaching God only concerning their infertility. The message, from the tradition's point of view, is that this was the way God signaled these women that they were not just accidental or incidental instruments that passed on the Jewish people's sacred calling from generation to generation. They were not marginal to the calling of the Jewish people. Rather, they were chosen, just as their husbands were chosen. Both mother and child, the stories seem to want to say, are thus touched by this intimate relationship with God.

Does this feel comforting? Is infertility too high a price to pay for such intimacy? Do you wish it could be otherwise? Perhaps you feel a mix of all these reactions. Be that as it may, we cannot help but take a moment to note that, of all of life's struggles, the Torah focuses so clearly on the pain and resolution of infertility in our founding mothers. At the very least, we know we are not alone.

Poems of fear, poems of hope

Round

Everything is round,
the apple and the plum,
the earth,
a drop,
the base of the tree,
the time of day and night,
times of the year,
and another thing,
every concept
is round,
and every deed,
if one looks deep enough.
The logical sequence itself
is a circle.
The return from going away
is the prize.
Birth and death,
laughter and weeping,
and then the understanding
that we cannot understand.

All right,
I will not discuss it anymore.
A round tear
drops from your eye.

RACHEL BOIMWALL

The Key

I am the garden locked,
a fountain sealed
a sealed-up spring. (Song of Songs 4:12)

Like the women in the Court of Avimelekh
my womb is stopped up.
There is no entry. (Gen. 20:18)

Once, while Rachel waited
God opened Leah's womb. (Gen. 29:31)
Still, while Rachel waited,
ten sons were born to Jacob.
Other people have children,
other women conceive.
Rachel waited
and we wait still.
We wait and search:
Are there mandrakes for us? (Gen. 30:14–16)

I know not what closes my womb.
Is it the spell of some long-ago wizard?
Is it the eye of an envious person?
Is it a scar from some once-endured illness?
The gift of a poisonous toxin?

Supplication

Three keys are in Your hand, God.
not entrusted to servants or agents:
the key of birthing,
the key of rain,
and the key of bringing the dead to life.

It is time for the key of birthing.
Bring it to us
to undo the lock.
Hear our prayer
open my womb,
for life.

TIKVA FRYMER-KENSKY

Reflections

What if there *were* hidden treasures of happiness kept in the vaults of heaven? And what if God offered you three keys, of all the keys in heaven, to have and to hold, and to put on your perpetual key ring? Which keys would you choose?

The keys I would love to have on my key ring are ...

Prayer to Rahmana

Rahmana is a feminized version of the words *rachum*, meaning merciful, *rachaman*, meaning merciful one, and *rechem*, meaning womb. One of God's most intimate and classic of names is *Harachaman*, used in times of distress and sadness. In the following meditation, writer Penina Adelman evokes this compassionate, feminine side of God. The prayer plays on Judaism's tradition of finding layers of meaning in a text and its letters. The words, the letters, the very breath used to speak the sounds reveal deeper, richer, simultaneous meanings.

Written in columns to represent layers of understanding, this prayer is to be read across, line by line. It builds upon the blessing given by Jacob to his son Joseph: "The God of your father will help you, *Shaddai* will bless you with the blessings of the heavens above and the blessings of the deep below; blessings of the breast and blessings of the womb." (Gen. 49:25) Penina meditated on each letter, and let the meanings unfold.

O Rahmana, Mother of Wombs

Mem is water	From the womb-waters of all my mothers
Alef begins	From the waters before the beginning
Lamed teaches	Teach me my genes:
Alef begins	How to grow a love seed
Bet is the house	In the cave of birth
Yod is the nipple	How to grow love in my breasts
Kaf receives	Teach me to receive with the hands of my womb.

O Rahmana, Mother of Wombs

Vav grows	Let the growth be steady
Yod is the nipple	Let fountains of warm milk flow
Ayin is the source	For the seed who lives in me
Zayin is male	Male or female
Resh recedes	Nestled in the
Kaf receives	Hands of my womb.
Vav grows	Let the growth be steady
Alef-tof is all	From beginning to ending
Shin flows	Rushing ceaselessly
Dalet-Yod	From my fountainous breasts.
Vav grows	Let every part of me grow
Yod opens	Let my mouth grow a singing rose
Bet is the house	Let my heart grow a blushing rose
Resh unfolds	Let my womb grow a shy rose
Kaf receives	Let my hands grow red roses

O Rahmana

Bet is the house	Make my womb a home of flesh and blood
Resh unfolds	For the tiny seed that needs a home,
Kaf contains	Put it deep inside
Vav-tof blooms	So it can grow to completion.
Mem is water	O womb-watering woman
Ayin-lamed resides	Plant this seed deep,

Bet is the house | Deep in my womb-waters
Resh unfolds | In my mother-waters
Kaf receives | Let my hands be leaves to carry the sun's warmth

Vav grows | Surging
Tof is completion | Fulfilling

Tof ends the beginning | The cycle of inhale
Hei breathes | And exhale
Vav grows | And the cycle of new life rising
Mem is water | From the deep hum.

O Rahmana, Mother of Wombs

Resh unfolds | Stretch out my womb
Bet is the house | Let this home keep growing
Tzadi knows | Let this wise river running through my breasts flow deep and wide

Tof is completion | Let the river run back to its source
Let my child teach me to be mother.

Tof is beginning | O, bring me back
Chet remembers | Remind me how to play in the ferns
Tof is completion | Again.

Bet is the house | Help my womb be ready
Resh unfolds | To hold new life
Kaf contains | In its hands
Vav unfolds | Swelling
Tof understands | To completion.

O Rahmana

Shin flows | In your warmth is a way
Dalet is the door | To the root of
Yod-mem is the sea | The deep
Vav is growing | To that frightening expanse
Resh is unfolding | That craves
Chet-mem is warm | The intimacies of water.

PENINA ADELMAN

If I had a son

Oh, if I had a son, a little son,
with black curled hair and clever eyes,
A little son to walk with in the garden
under morning skies
a son,
a little son.

I'd call him Uri, little laughing Uri,
a tender name, as light, as full of joy
as sunlight on the dew, as tripping on the tongue
as the laughter of a boy—
"Uri"
I'd call him.

And still I wait, as mother Rachel waited,
or Hannah at Shiloh, she the barren one,
until the day comes when my lips whisper,
"Uri, my son."

RAHEL BLUWSTEIN

Prayers and rituals for a Friday night

Shabbat candles open a portal to heaven. And in heaven, hidden away beneath the Throne of Glory, concealed from worldly sight, is the primordial light from the first day of creation. The Torah tells us that the first of God's creations was light. Yet, the sun and the moon were made on day four. Where, then, did the first light come from? The rabbis say it is a supernal light, an extra-ordinary light, a light of such great power and clarity that it illumines the universe from one end to the other. It is, however, too pure and too powerful for the eyes of humankind. We must wait to see it in the World to Come. Therefore, before creating Adam and Eve, God hid the light away. However, every week, a few rays of this light are released, brought back into the world through the flames of the Shabbat candles. For the holiness of Shabbat that flows into our world is itself from the World to Come.

This, then, is a most auspicious time for prayer. For centuries, women have tarried over Shabbat candlelighting, petitioning God on behalf of their families, themselves, and the people Israel. At candlelighting time, they feel just a bit closer to heaven. So can we.

A prayer to be said upon candlelighting

The couple lights the candles and says:

> *El Malei Rachamim*, God full of grace and caring, we seek Your face in our time of darkness. Shine Your light of love and compassion upon us. Open before us the gates of prayers and tears, for we come before You laden with both.
>
> Help us, this month, conceive a child. Select for us a holy seed, a child who will grow strong and healthy, sweet and caring.
>
> Command Your angels to watch over us, and to be with us as helpers and guides.
>
> Hear our plea, for You alone hold the key to life.
>
> Just as You heard the cry of our ancestors, Sarah, Rebecca, Rachel, Leah, and Hannah, so may You remember us.

Woman continues alone:

> God of all creation, You have made the angels above and humans below. Angels do not eat, do not sleep, do not bear children, and do not die. Women eat, sleep, bear children, and die. If I am an angel, then let me live forever. But if I am a woman, let me bear a child.

Together:

> Do not hide Your face from us, Merciful One. We ask for your help, God. We ask You for hope. Please, give us a child. Amen.

*Barukh ata adonai eloheinu melekh ha'olam, asher kiddeshanu b'mitzvotav
v'tzivanu l'hadlik neir shel Shabbat.*

Blessed are you, God of all creation, who sanctifies us
through Your commandments and commands us to light the
Shabbat candles.

We can only imagine the ways that Sarah, Rachel, and Leah spoke
to God in their search for a child. But tradition offers a weave of
prayers around Hannah. Hannah was the beloved wife of Elka-
nah. In her desire to have a child, she suffered twice—the distress of her infertility and the silent taunting of her co-wife's
fertility. Her husband tried to soothe her pain, telling her that
his love matched the blessing of ten children. But she would not
be comforted.

So when Hannah joined her family on their annual pilgrimage to the local shrine in Shiloh, she approached God and
offered this promise on her own behalf: "If you will look upon
the heartache of your humble servant, and remember me, and
not forget me, if you will give me a child, I will dedicate him to
the Lord all the days of his life." (1 Sam. 11) Those are all the
words that the Bible records, but the text tells us she kept on
praying.

What else did she pray? the rabbis asked. And as is the way
of midrash, they offered an answer to their own question. She
spoke to God about humans and angels, they said, and the difference in character endowed to each. This is the prayer appear-
ing in the meditation above. And she spoke about barrenness,
arguing that it is an assault not just against her, but against the
very elegance of God's worldly design:

"Dear God, You created everything in a woman's body for a
purpose. Our eyes You made for seeing, our ears for hearing,
our noses for smelling, our mouths for eating and speaking,

our hands for working. And You have made our breasts for
nursing. Yet what good are my breasts, God? Give me a child
so that I may nurse with them."

Hannah is depicted as bold and clever. Both of her rabbinically
authored prayers speak of her barrenness in cosmic terms, as a vio-
lation of God's world. To give Hannah a child, then, is not merely to heal one woman, but to heal the world.

The rabbis offer yet one more appeal by Hannah, couching
her request in the form of a parable: "Master of the Universe, You
have hosts upon hosts of creatures in your world. Is it so hard to
give me one child? It is like an earthly king who makes a feast for
his servants. A man comes by, poor and hungry, and asks the servants for a piece of bread. They ignore him. So the man goes to
the king and says: 'Your majesty, with all the food you have, you
cannot spare one slice of bread?'"

So moving was Hannah's biblical prayer for a child, a mother's plea to overcome her infertility, that it became the liturgical
model upon which the rabbis based the Eighteen Benedictions,
the central prayer of every Jewish service.

Another prayer to be said by the husband and wife when they light Shabbat candles

Paired lights proclaim the miracle,
A straight line defined;
The shortest distance to You, O Eternal,
A clear path, a comet's flight.

So our praises rise to You,
A shining line lifts from paired lights,
Piercing the darkness,
Illuminating dark clouds.

Morning and evening we praise You;
In our going and coming back,

Our awakening and sleeping,
In our search and return, we praise Your Name.

In the duality of our days,
In the right and the left,
The twinned longings and givings,
We remember the lights and praise You.

We follow the straight line to You,
From here to an unknown there,
Believing and following,
Through obstacles, unwavering.

DEBBIE PERLMAN

Wine ritual for Friday nights

In earlier rabbinic times, wine was stored concentrated, much too thick and strong to be drunk straight from the jug. Accordingly, before drinking, the wine had to be mixed with water to give it its proper dilution. In the Jewish mystical tradition, red wine represents the divine attribute of *din*, judgment, whereby God judges us strictly according to our merits. Water represents the divine attribute of *chesed*, unconditional kindness, whereby God deals with us according to God's boundless graciousness. During the course of every week, each attribute vies with the other, seeking its own ascendancy. But on Friday nights, *din* is weakened, constrained by the enveloping presence of *chesed*. We can further strengthen the hand of *chesed* by mixing water or white wine with the deep red wine. This ritual mixing is said to be especially beneficial for women who have suffered miscarriages. The couple then drinks the mixture, toasting *l'chayyim*—to life.

Reflections

Families come in all shapes and sizes. Family rituals strengthen bonds and celebrate moments that otherwise might be taken for granted or forgotten. Talk about your Friday night traditions.

On Friday nights we tend to ...

One of our favorite red wines is ...

One of our favorite white wines is ...

Two good wines to mix are ...

(You may also want to try one of the new pomegranate wines, symbolizing beauty and fertility.)

A prayer I would like to say on Friday nights is ...

This week we are grateful for ...

For this coming week we hope ...

Prayers for a childless man

Most modern infertility prayers are written for and by women. But men suffer infertility too, both in body and in spirit. Some men may respond with aloofness and a minimum of lost equilibrium. Others may seek to plow through their hurt or bury it deep within their work. Still others privately admit to a deep anguish. Whatever the response, this prayer is for men, authored by men, in the classic blend of humble yet bold petition.

> *Av Harachaman*, merciful father, God of all creation, remember Your children who seek children of their own. Bless them with the ability to give life to a child, and grant me the happiness of creating a child with my beloved wife, [her name] daughter of [her mother's name]. Let us fulfill the mitzvah: "Be fruitful and multiply." (Gen. 1:28) Remember what is written in the Torah, "There will not be among you a barren man or a barren woman." (Deut. 7:14) And "No one will miscarry or be barren in your land." (Exod. 23:26) Make these promises come true for us. And if You cannot grant us this blessing out of merit, then grant it to us out of mercy.
>
> Change our destiny for the better. Remember us with a child, along with all those who suffer infertility, just as You remembered our ancestors of long ago. And if there is a blemish or obstacle that prevents this conception, heal us and we will be healed, for You, God, are the healer of all flesh. *Avinu Malkeinu*, our father, our protector, do not ignore my plea. Do not turn away from my tears. Fill our home with children's laughter, and my heart with a father's joy. Merciful Father, listen to my voice. For You are God, who hears my prayers.

Another prayer for a man to say before joining with his wife

May it be Your will, my God and God of my ancestors, that a child be conceived tonight from this drop that comes from me. Let it be a healthy child, a child blessed with goodness and length of days. May the child live a long, holy, and noble life, be prosperous and wise, according to Your will. So may it be with this child, and all our grandchildren and great-grandchildren to come.

Reflections

We all want to bring our children into a world of peace and prosperity, possibilities and growth. Yet the world needs so much help to be ready for our children.

While we can never make it perfect, we can make it better, for ourselves and for all children, everywhere. To help make this happen, we promise to [*name one achievable goal*] this week.

Sacred union: a prayer from the tradition to be said before sexual relations

In the world of kabbalah, the expansive, centuries-old tradition of Jewish mysticism, all intentional behavior in this earthly world affects the status of the heavenly world above. In this cosmology, the Shekhinah is the feminine aspect of God, the earthly presence of the One who is beyond all. She is also a forlorn lover, in exile, separated from her source, her center, the Holy One blessed be He. She is eager to return home and be reunited with the Eternal One, *Ein Sof*. This, however, can only happen when the world ceases to be in exile, and that can only happen with the help of humankind through the proper performance of the commandments. Any mitzvah, properly done, can speed the reunion of the Shekhinah and the Holy One, blessed be He. But the most potent way to bring God and the Shekhinah together is through sacred and holy sexual relations between husband and wife.

The following prayer, or *kavvanah*, inspired by the mystical beliefs of kabbalah, is to be said before the act of love. It asks God to help the husband and wife conceive a child, even as the husband and wife are helping the Shekhinah and God enact their reunion.

> In the name of the Holy One, blessed be He, and His Shekhinah, in prayer and for mercy, for the sake of the union of the first two letters of God's ineffable name, *Yod Hei,* with the last two letters of God's ineffable name, *Vav Hei,* a complete and total union, for the sake of all Israel, we are ready and prepared for the mitzvah of relations; of joining together, pressing body to body, as it is written in the Torah, "and the man cleaved to his wife, and they were as one flesh. . . ." (Gen. 2:24) Dear God and God of our ancestors, give us the strength, ability, and readiness at this moment of relations to continue to bring your abundant flow of blessings from the World Above to all the worlds below, and into our souls and spirits as well, just as Rachel and Leah merited it when the two of them built the House of Israel, raising righteous, wise, healthy sons. Let us, too, merit bearing and raising wise, healthy, strong children, well into old age; and let us rejoice in them and their children.
>
> And just as You blessed Jacob and Leah, as it says, "And he lay with her that night, and God heard Leah's prayers, and she conceived and gave birth to her fifth son . . ." (Gen. 30:16–17) so may this moment be one of blessing for us. May it be Your will to help us and aid us in this very union.

Segulot: *fertility folkways*

"Rabbi Yitzchak said: Four things annul the harsh decree: *tzedakah,* fervent prayer, changing one's name, and changing one's ways."

Over the centuries, communities of Jews developed complementary methods of healing designed to improve their chances of conception and healthy pregnancies. While differing one from the other, most of these methods were founded on one of two fundamental

beliefs: one, that God guides the affairs of each individual according to God's will and wisdom, and that by changing oneself or one's
way, one can influence God's will; or two, that certain powerful,
causal, and metaphysical conditions operate in the world, such as the
arrangement of the stars and the jealousy of evil spirits. By affect-
ing, or outsmarting, these conditions, one can alter one's destiny.

Tzedakah

Someone once visited the Chafetz Chayyim, a pious sage of the
early twentieth century known especially for his caring and his
simplicity. The visitor was seeking advice on sympathetic rituals
that would ensure his fertility. The Chafetz Chayyim said, "I do
not have any such knowledge, but I will tell you this: choose one
act of kindness to tend to here in the city, and perhaps God will
reward you for caring for the needs of others . . ." Three years
later, the visitor had a son. As Abraham prayed for the household
of Avimelekh, so the visitor cared for the needs of the community. And both were rewarded.

Therefore, our tradition offers the following advice on giving
tzedakah. The couple desiring a child should provide for the needs
of the students and study-partners who gather at night in the
synagogue, giving them sufficient water to drink and candles for
light. "What can a man do to ensure that he will have children?
Rabbi Eliezer said: Generously distribute his money to the poor."
So, every Friday night, the woman should also place a few coins in
her *tzedakah* box. And whenever they can, the husband and wife
should give generously to those in need.

The curing of infertility through the gift of *tzedakah* is no
guarantee. Even the Chafetz Chayyim said, "Perhaps." But if we
cannot speak of the certainty of curing, we can speak of the possibility of healing. *Psychologically,* giving *tzedakah* makes us feel better about ourselves and encourages us to focus on the other parts

of ourselves that are able to give life. Caring about another chips away at the veneer of unworthiness that may have begun to form over our self-esteem and allows us to once again feel worthy of a child and meritorious of God's kindness. Considering the ways we can engage in *tzedakah* allows us to move out of our private sphere of pain and tend to the pain that surrounds others in need. *Symbolically,* *tzedakah* enables us to model the kind of unconditional kindness we now seek from God. *Communally,* it unites us with our ancestors who gave *tzedakah* throughout the millennia seeking mercy and beneficence for themselves and their loved ones. *Emotionally,* giving *tzedakah* in a moment of pain and sorrow connects us to others at a time we seek to retire and crawl deep inside of our own enveloping sorrow. And *practically,* giving *tzedakah* helps another person in need. "*Tzedakah* saves a person from death," our tradition tells us.

Reflections

Organizations or causes I helped last year include ...

Organizations or causes I hope to help this year include ...

I choose these groups because ...

I help these groups by ...

Ritual for changing one's name

Changing one's name is an age-old Jewish practice meant to fool destiny and improve one's future. The new name is a permanent refiguring, a patina that covers and colors the identity of the individual. The person is no longer who they once were. The new name confers upon them a new identity. It is the one they will use when they are called to the Torah and the name that will one day be etched above their graves. The foundation of this ritual is the belief that illness and infertility are decreed from on high, stamped for delivery with the recipient's name. If a certain individual is called by a new name, the decree becomes undeliverable—and therefore ineffectual. To be granted a new name confers feelings of release, safety, promise, and hope.

For those intrigued by this classic ritual of renewal, a few words of advice are in order: "Changing one's name is not to be undertaken lightly. It requires much deliberation and guidance regarding when to change the name, how to change it, and which new names to choose. To tamper with name changing may upset the person's good fortune and damage their future. For changing one's name changes one's soul, and we don't do this lightly. When a child is born and parents select this name for that child, that name did not come into their minds accidentally. God put it in their minds and mouths, appropriate for that child's soul. And it is written in Aravei Nahal that the letters of a person's name are the vessels that bring the flow of the divine to them."

In the past, an entirely new name would be substituted for the old. Today, we are more likely to add new names. The new name can either reflect images of healing and compassion, like Raphael or Raphaelah and Nachum or Nechamah, or it may be selected randomly by opening the Bible and adopting the first name one sees (providing it is suitable both in association and gender). The new name then becomes the person's first name.

The person charged with naming the individual stands before two witnesses and recites:

> Our rabbis taught that changing one's name alters one's destiny. God changed Sarah's name from Sarai and Abraham's name from Abram, in both cases adding the letter *hei*, which designates the name of God, thus enabling them to conceive Isaac. We therefore gather for the purpose of adding a name to the one formerly known as [person's name]. He/she is a new person now, and if a decree was uttered for [person's former name], it is not decreed for [person's new name], for this is a different person. May the new name serve as a fresh vessel, offering [person's new name] an unimpeded flow of God's divine kindness. And may it soon bring the news that a child will be born to [person's new name].

Reflections

The story behind my given name is ...

To me, my new name means ...

I chose the new name because ...

My new name makes me feel ...

3

Prayers for the Holidays

The holidays can be especially difficult times for those seeking a child. Families gather in multiple generations. Grandparents enjoy the presence of their grandchildren; grandchildren
enjoy the presents from their grandparents. The shouts of nieces
and nephews fighting, laughing, and conspiring waft through the
house. The synagogue is suddenly filled with young families,
broods in tow. With joy in the air and children all around, childless couples and those seeking another child, can feel distanced
from their community just at the moment they most desire to be
drawn in and comforted.

Over the centuries, folk traditions have developed that
acknowledge this desire for connection and caring. Images, symbols, lessons, and stories of these holidays are turned into vehicles
that transport the prayers of couples trying for a child.

The prayers and rituals presented below are samples culled
from a variety of classical traditions as well as from more modern
liturgical creations. Each of these was born of the need to join

the petitioner's personal desires to the themes and sentiments of the national celebration. They can be used as presented or can serve as models upon which to base the creation of your own rituals and prayers.

Prayers for Rosh Hashanah

Rosh Hashanah is the birthday of the world, a time when the air is touched with the scent of creation, a time when everything is filled with newness, hope, and possibility. It was on Rosh Hashanah, the rabbis say, that God remembered the longings of Sarah, Rachel, and Hannah (Rosh Hashanah 11a), and they conceived not long thereafter. Such an association turns Rosh Hashanah into a propitious and proper time to place our prayers for a child before God.

A prayer for the woman to say on the first night of Rosh Hashanah when she lights the candles

Creator of the World, You answered the prayers of our matriarchs Sarah, Rachel, and Hannah during this month of Tishrei. You listened to their pleas and opened their wombs, helped them conceive and brought them to a healthy birth. So may You answer me, too. On this, the day that celebrates the birth of the world, remember me. My God and God of my ancestors, be gracious unto me. Let me conceive this year with my beloved, and let the child who comes from this union be endowed with a soul of gentleness and holiness. Let no harm come to me all the months of my pregnancy. Let me give birth at a good time, a proper time. May my beloved and I merit the pleasure of raising our child in health and happiness, together. So may it be Your will.

A prayer for the couple to say
on the second night of Rosh Hashanah

It is a well-known Rosh Hashanah custom to take a bit of apple, dip it in honey, and ask God for a good and sweet new year. This is a remnant of an age-old tradition in which we once ate many ritual foods on Rosh Hashanah, representative of the dreams we hoped would come true in the coming year. Sometimes the connection between the food and the desire was linguistic, playing on the closeness of sounds between the name of the one and the words describing the other (as if upon eating a *turnip* one would say: may blessings *turn up* wherever I go). Sometimes the connection was found in the property of the food, like the sweetness of honey; or in the food's symbolism, as with fish and fertility, or round foods and the renewal of life. The modern couple seeking to be blessed with a child may reclaim this tradition by eating a pomegranate, a fruit storied with tales of love and fertility, and already associated with Rosh Hashanah. In many families, the pomegranate serves as the new food it is customary to eat on the second night of the New Year, enabling us to recite again the *she-hecheyanu*, the blessing of appreciation, of being grateful for this moment that we are able to enjoy together.

At dinner, the husband and wife open the pomegranate and each selects a choice seed from the fruit. Before eating, the woman says:

> "God, as I chose a seed from this round, luscious fruit, so You too choose a seed from me. Plant it deep in my body, and give it time to grow. When it is ripe, let it spill forth from me, whole and healthy and full of life. So may it be Your will."

The man says:

> "God, as I chose a seed from this round, red fruit, may You choose to join my seed with my wife's. Let the joy of our love

mingle and bring forth fruit of its own. This year, may we be blessed with a child. So may it be Your will."

Barukh ata adonai eloheinu melekh ha'olam, borei pri ha'eitz.

Blessed are You, God of all creation, who creates the fruit of the tree.

Barukh ata adonai eloheinu melekh ha'olam, shehecheyanu, v'kiyimanu, v'higiyanu laz'man hazeh.

Blessed are You, God of all creation, who has sustained us, cared for us, and brought us to this moment.

New Year's compote—second night

Pink grapefruits, navel oranges, and pomegranates combine to make a Rosh Hashanah version of a classic Ashkenazi dessert: compote. The fruit of the New Year blends with comfortable memories of our grandmothers' kitchens, serving up helpings of hope and connection. Cut citrus fruit into bite-size pieces. Roll the pomegranate between your hands to soften. Open it and add the seeds to the fruit slices. In a saucepan, combine white wine and sherry with brown sugar and honey to desired sweetness. Heat mixture until the sugar is dissolved. Scoop the fruit into a bowl and cover with the syrup. Serve cold.

Reflections

My favorite memory from last year is ...

The one thing I would do differently if I could is ...

I am different now from last year in this way ...

What I hope for most this coming year is ...

Prayers to be said between Rosh Hashanah and Yom Kippur

The nine months of pregnancy find resonance in this holiday season. There are nine days from Rosh Hashanah to Yom Kippur, and nine occurrences of God's name in Hannah's prayer of thanksgiving that we read as the haftarah on Rosh Hashanah. The Hebrew letter for nine, *tet*, written in script looks like a profile of a pregnant belly. In the following ritual, every day of these nine days of renewal and repentance the couple recites a line from the tradition that recalls the mystery and the joy of childbirth.

The recitation of these verses can be accompanied by the giving of *tzedakah* (a dollar amount equal to the day count), or they may be recited when the couple settles into bed.

Day 1 (first night of Rosh Hashanah):

> There are three keys that the Holy One entrusts to no one else but are kept always in the divine hand. They are: the key of rain, the key of eternal life, and the key of the womb. Please God, on this anniversary of the birth of the world, remember the key, open Your hand, and give us a child.

Day 2 (second night of Rosh Hashanah):

> We do not know the way the spirit of life enters the one that lies within the womb of a woman. And we cannot understand the deeds of God, the One who is the author of all. (Eccles. 11:5) But please, God, visit this miracle upon us and give us a child.

Day 3:

> My dove, in the cranny of the rocks, hidden by the cliff, let me see your face, let me hear your voice, for your voice is sweet and your face is sweet. (Song of Songs 2:14) We await the voice of our own little one. Please, God, give us a child.

Day 4:

> Sing, barren one . . . for the time has come to expand the length of your tent. Let the drapes of your dwelling billow out. (Isa. 54:1–2) Please, God, make this call come true for us. Remember us and give us a child.

Day 5:

> Unless the Lord builds the house, it is built in vain (Ps. 127:1) for it takes three to build a household: a man, a woman and the Holy One. Please, God, remember us and give us a child.

Day 6:

> And God remembered Rachel, heard her cries, and opened her womb. (Gen. 30:22) Hear us too, God, and give us a child.

Day 7:

> The God of your father will help you. *Shaddai* will bless you. Blessing will flow from above, and blessings will flow from below. Blessings of the breast and blessings of the womb. (Gen. 49:25) We await our blessings, God. Give us a child.

Day 8:

> They shall not labor and produce nothing. They shall not give birth in vain. For their children shall be the blessed ones of God, and their children shall always be with them. (Isa. 65:23) We long to be among the blessed ones, God. Please, give us a child.

Day 9:

> The soul is Yours, the body Your creation; have compassion on Your creation. We will care tenderly for the one entrusted to us. Please, God, give us a child.

Prayers and rituals for Sukkot

Hospitality

One of the grand traditions of Sukkot is having guests, both real and imagined, visit in our *sukkot*. Many Jews who build *sukkot* are careful to invite family and friends to join with them. Others invite exotic guests from the past: Abraham, Isaac, Jacob, Joseph, Moses, Aaron, David and Solomon, Sarah, Rebecca, Rachel, Leah, Miriam, Hannah, Deborah. Taking someone as a guest into your home is not just a seasonal tradition. It is also one of the remedies against infertility. The Shunamite woman became pregnant after caring for Elisha, the itinerant prophet, and Sarah conceived after providing for the three nameless visitors. It is as if to say, "Just as we offer temporary shelter within the walls of our home to the ones in need, so may we merit offering temporary shelter within the walls of our womb to the one we desire."

As we invite guests into our home on Sukkot, we can turn to God and say,

> "God, even as we welcome these guests into this temporary home of ours, and tend to them and feed them and send them gently on their way, so may You make a temporary home in our womb for our child, and tend to her and feed her and when the time is right, send her gently on her way."

Biting the *pitom*

A classic post-Sukkot ritual designed to encourage conception is for the woman to bite off the stem of the *etrog* (called the *pitom*), one of the fruits used in the rituals of the holiday. She is to do this on Hoshana Rabbah, after the *etrog* is used for the last time, for without the stem it is not ritually fit. The rabbis say that the forbidden fruit that Eve ate in the Garden of Eden was the *etrog*.

By biting off the stem, the woman makes restitution for Eve's disobedience, as if to say: If I had been there in the Garden, I would not have eaten of the fruit; so please reward me with my desire, a child.

Loosing the band of the *lulav*

Binding the myrtle and the willow to the *lulav* is a small band, a strand of the palm tied in a knot. Infertility is often imagined to be a tying up or binding up of the tubes and womb of the woman. On the last day of Sukkot, the woman can take the *lulav* and unbind the knot that holds the *lulav* together. As she does this, she may say:

> God, every day we say, Blessed are You God, who heals the sick, restores strength to the weary, and releases those who are bound. As I untie the band on this *lulav*, God, untie the knot that prevents me from conceiving. Release me, too, from the bonds of sadness. Blessed are You, God, source of life and hope.

Geshem: verses for our mothers

In Israel, the rains come only in the winter. A year's worth of water must fall and be gathered and stored in those six months. The rainy season arrives just after the fall harvest, marked by the holiday of Sukkot. On Shemini Atzeret, therefore, the holiday that immediately follows the last day of Sukkot, an extraordinary prayer for rain, called *Geshem*, is said. It reminds God of our patriarchs who performed acts of piety with and through water, and how we, through our ancestral association with them, also merit the blessings of water.

Those who seek a child also seek the blessings of water. Water is the medium of life. It was from the waters of the deep that all life came. It is within the waters of our body that new life is formed. It is out of the waters of our body that new life is born.

The prayer below, modeled on the structure of *Geshem* and created by Mark Frydenberg and translated by Rabbi Simchah Roth, was modified slightly for our needs. It reminds God of the ways that our foremothers preserved life through their use of water, and how we too, through association with them, merit the life-giving blessings of water.

Sarah:

Remember the barren one who offered the three strangers water [Gen. 18:2]

At a time when she ceased to be as living waters [Gen. 18:11]

And God remembered her in her old age, in her womb creating water [Gen. 21:1]

For her sake, don't hold back the life that comes from water.

Rebecca:

Remember the kind one who carried a pitcher of water [Gen. 24:13]

To the servant she gave water [Gen. 24:17]

In Haran for the camels, she drew water [Gen. 24:19]

For her sake, don't hold back the life that comes from water.

Rachel:

Remember the younger one who to the flock of Lavan gave water [Gen. 29:10]

Her lover kissed her near the well of water [Gen. 29:11]

At Ramah for her children, her eyes weep tears of water [Lam. 1:16]

For her sake, don't hold back the life that comes from water.

Leah:

Remember the Mother of Children who at Yabbok was first
to cross the water [Gen. 32:23]

Her eyes were tender from crying tears of water [Gen. 29:17]

Her son lived out his days at the edge of the water [Gen.
49:13]

For her sake, don't hold back the life that comes from water.

Miriam:

Remember the sister who watched the baby crying in the
water [Exod. 2:6]

She sang and rejoiced after the people Israel crossed the
water [Exod. 15:20]

In Kadesh she was buried near gurgling water [Num. 20:1]

For her sake, don't hold back the life that comes from
water.

Etrog jelly

Eating jelly made from the flesh of the *etrog* is considered salutary
for women wanting children. So, after Sukkot, some women boil
the *etrog* in water and sugar and prepare it to eat on Tu B'shevat.
Eating an *etrog* is said to be good for women who are pregnant.
Even more, a woman having difficulty giving birth was sometimes
given a raw *etrog* to bite upon, with the hope that the bitterness
of the fruit would distract her from the pain of her travail. Biting
the *etrog* might also have been a magical remedy against the pain,
employing the formula of fighting fire with fire. Since it was eating the *etrog*, the forbidden fruit of the Garden of Eden according
to some rabbis, that brought on the curse of pain in childbirth,
only a bite of the *etrog* can dull the pain.

Song for Hanukkah

Hanukkah is the holiday of lights, of believing that we can lift the darkness that sometimes bears in around us. Hanukkah is also a holiday of rededication when husband and wife can renew their devotion to each other. Hanukkah is eight days; the Song of Songs, the great love poem of the Bible, is eight chapters. Each night, after lighting the Hanukkah candles, join with your loved one and together read one chapter of the Song of Songs.

Reflections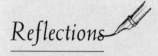

Hanukkah is a time of miracles and light.

The kind of miracles I believe in are ...

I can be a source of light for others by ...

Prayer for Tu B'shevat

Tu B'shevat is the birthday of the trees. In the days of the Temple, Jewish farmers thanked God for the goodness of the earth by bringing sacrifices to Jerusalem commensurate with the size of their harvest. When measuring their yield, they needed to know which fruits belonged to which year. To help them in their assessment, tradition determined that all fruits that ripened after Tu B'shevat would be counted for the following year.

Tu B'shevat, then, is considered the start of the growing season, a time when the sap is said to begin to rise, a propitious time to approach God for help.

On Tu B'shevat, the couple seeking a child may plant a fruit tree (in colder climes it may be necessary to begin it indoors). Or they may choose to plant aloe in the house or the yard. Aloe is a tree whose sap is used for healing cuts and wounds. It is a hardy plant that grows many arms, and if one is cut, either by accident or to harvest the sap inside, it can be rooted readily to begin a new plant.

When planting, the couple may offer their own prayers, or say:

> "God, on this new year's day, we plant this tree and wait for its blossoming. So, too, may You help us plant a tree of life from the seeds of our love, and await with us the season of its blossoming. As it says, 'Though they walk with tears, bearing their sacks of seed, they will return in joy, carrying their sheaves of grain.'" (Ps. 126:6)

Ritual for Passover

The Jewish people was born on Passover. In Egypt, we were but a cluster of souls in exile. During the Exodus, we became a people. The images tell us so. We were delivered from Mitzrayim, a narrow place. We passed through the tight canal of the Red Sea, whose waters rushed apart with the help of God. We emerged on dry land, tired and spent, but healthy and sound. And we let out a cry of gladness and song.

At the seder, the *afikomen* is the symbol of birth. The *afikomen* is the piece of matzah hidden at the beginning of the meal, found by the children, and brought forth by them in return for a handsome ransom, for the seder is not complete until the *afikomen* is eaten.

Why is the *afikomen* the symbol of fertility? For two reasons. First, numerically, the letters of the word *afikomen* equal the letters of the words *ken yirbu*, may your progeny multiply. Second, in some Jewish traditions it was the custom to write or repetitively recite variations of the word *pok*, meaning "go forth," when a woman was in labor. In Hebrew, *pok* and *-fik-* are functionally equivalent, and *afik omen* can be taken to mean "I will bring forth a person." Just as the *afikomen* is hidden and then brought forth from hiding by the children, so the woman who eats the *afikomen* as the last food of the seder hopes she will be blessed with bringing forth a child from her most hidden place.

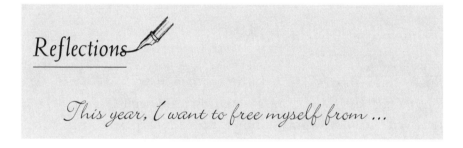

Reflections

This year, I want to free myself from ...

Shavuot

At midnight on Shavuot, the holiday that celebrates the giving of the Torah on Mt. Sinai so many years ago, the heavens are said to open. The veils that separate God and humanity are pulled back. Energies and communication flow smoothly between the worlds. It is an awesome, auspicious time for prayer. To help us stay awake and focused throughout the night, to help us recapture the intimacy of that covenantal meeting between God and the Jewish people, we study Torah with our family and friends.

Study itself is an act of intimacy and an act of creation. It is an act of intimacy, for through study we enter the mind and thoughts of the one we are studying. And it is an act of creation, for through our attention, their words become animated once again. Teaching what one has studied extends the act of creation, for teaching enlivens the one who is taught. And so it is seen by our tradition: "Whoever teaches Torah to another is considered as though he formed him." (Tosefta Horayot 2:7)

On this evening, then, the couple may invite family and friends to join them in an evening of study. The first chapters of Genesis, which speak of creation, may be rich texts to study. To help everyone stay awake, serve round finger food, including cut fruit salad marinated in grenadine—a juice made from pomegranates.

Prayer for Rosh Chodesh

Rosh Chodesh is the first day of the new month, a time of new beginnings. On this day, new enterprises are begun, old hopes are renewed. The following petition is a blending of two classic texts: a prayer recited by Italian Jewish women on the evening they went to the *mikveh*, their monthly ritual bath, and a prayer that is said when announcing the new month. This petition may be recited on any night of the month, but is especially well suited for Rosh Chodesh.

> Dear God, gracious source of hope, answer me this month. Just as You remembered my mother Sarah when she longed for a child, remember me. Just as You answered my mother Rebecca when she sought You in need, answer me. Just as You cared for my mother Rachel when her empty arms ached, care for me. Just as you listened to Hannah when she cried to You, listen to me.

God, accept my prayer, and grant my heart's desires. And even as You remember me now, so may You remember all the men and women who long for a child tonight.

May it be Your will my God, that You renew our lives this coming month. May it be a month of goodness and blessing, healing and vitality, fruitfulness and abundance, joy and happiness, deliverance and consolation, for me, my husband/wife, the people Israel, and all the inhabitants of the world.

4

Mourning Loss

Another period. A pregnancy lost. A child stillborn. Different paths toward emptiness—all devastating.

Even if we try to pray, our prayers often crumble in our souls, our dreams dissolve in our hearts. Despair seeps in the doors, taps at the windows, and threatens to clog all our passages of hope. How can we speak softly to God when we see, yet again, the fruitless stain of our blood; when we feel the lifeless mass slipping from our wombs; or when we hold a beautiful, perfect but still child in our arms? For some of us, no amount of explanation—medical or theological—can soothe.

We hurt; we cry. We are angry, scared, and lonely. Which feeling do we express first?

Anger?

"Is this the way You answer us, God?" we may want to cry out. "Were not our prayers and tears good enough? Is there some unredeemable failing in us? Our bodies are now empty, but our hearts are full, all stopped up, blocked and bloated with love.

Where shall we send it, God? Where shall we find relief? Release Your love so we may release ours."

Fear?

"God, in You I seek my refuge; in You I place my hope. Will I never be a mother? Will I never hold my child in my arms? Deliver me from these terrors. You are a shield about me, the staff that helps me stand upright. I call to You, God. Answer me. I lie down to sleep. God, stay with me throughout the night and be with me when the dawn breaks."

Blame? Shame? Confusion? Despair? Dread? All these feelings may swirl, intermingled, around us.

In this chapter are prayers, meditations, and rituals of comfort and healing that speak to the variety of responses we experience after a loss.

The stain

For most of our lives, we look upon the punctuality of our monthly flow as a sign of health and vigor, sometimes even a blessing, especially if we have been a bit careless in our sexual encounters. And in our more contemplative moments, despite the discomfort or nuisance our periods may cause us, we recognize the awesome and sacred power that dwells within our bodies, how our inner cycles open us to the eternal cycles of life beyond ourselves. We can imagine our heartbeat, our breath, as part of the murmuring chorus of the universe.

But when we seek to have a child, the blood that flows from between our legs becomes a sign of failure, of sadness, of emptiness, of death. It begins with a spot, which stains our garments and our spirit. And we wonder, will we ever get it out?

Tapping a Stone

A coin, a shard, a pot, a lamp.
An archeologist explains how our world's
best secrets are the hardest to find.
Like him we believed in buried treasures,
thought we could, under the smooth terrain
of my naked body, find that one dark cave
where our waters run.
After all, we had the map, knew the rules,
charted the peaks and valleys of our indigenous territory,
and every evening before a full-length mirror
we'd find one more clue to convince us.
But somehow we were wrong,
the parched earth didn't yield,
the small brown smudge of the pregnancy test
signaled only a river gone dry.
Beneath every stone a story.

JANE SCHAPIRO

A prayer for a woman in search of comfort

Dear God, you made the world overflowing with water, with streams and rivers that nourish the earth, pools and ponds that teem with life.

But not me. I am like a wadi; I fill up and empty to no purpose. Nothing is held by me, nothing nourished.

That is not the way it should be.

My arms ache under the burden of their emptiness; my breasts long to be full.

It is You, God, who causes the day to break, assigning dawn its place in the east. It is You, God, who sets the world on its course, guiding its paths as it glides through the heavens. It is You, God, who closed the sea behind doors when it burst forth out of the womb; who clothed the new waters, swaddling them in dense clouds. (from Job 38)

You know the joy of birth. Can You share a bit with me?

I too want to clothe my children in clouds and swaddle them
in love.
    Hear me, God, for You hear the prayers of the broken-
hearted.
    Be with me, God. In my search for a child, I will look
toward You.

The Bath

Each month I find the red surprise of death,
and I fear for us.
How few we are, how much grayer,
how much fine dust we wasted as we lived for ourselves.
In the darkness I light a candle
and remember the moon's promise to women.

What then of the bath and its power?
Suppose the ritual of waiting and water and joining
under the velvet tent of night
might conjure the desired coincidence,
the union of inner bride and inner groom.
I think it would be the same miracle by which our half souls
    first met.

Each month I walk in the garden of the new moon,
dreaming of fullness, of our moment of union.
Thinking of unhappiness and happiness in their turns,
of freshness, hope, and many chances.

LYNN E. LEVIN

Mourning miscarriage

The law may wait until we bring forth a child to call us mothers.
But we know better. The moment that magic wand we purchase
from the pharmacy reveals to us that one plus one made three,
hope flares. In that moment, we become mothers. Our bodies, our
spirits, make room for another. And we lovingly, gratefully, sur-

render ourselves to it. We know now that we are a partner in eternity. Nothing is more precious, nothing more important.

And then—it slips away. Whether at home in wave after wave of that rush of red, or at the hospital in one sterile whoosh. The loss drains us. We are spent. "You can go back to work tomorrow," the doctors may tell us. But we cannot. We held life, but gave birth to death, and now we need time to recover.

We no longer breathe the same air as everyone else. The world belongs to them, not us. Joy is drained from our bodies. We cry until we can cry no more. We are angry, at ourselves, our spouses, life, doctors, medicine, God, all pregnant women, happy mothers.

Healing after a miscarriage

Nothing helps. I taste ashes
in my mouth. My eyes are flat,
dead. I want no platitudes,
no stupid shallow comfort.
I hate all pregnant women,
all new mothers, all soft babies.

The space I'd made inside myself
where I'd moved over
to give my beloved room to grow—
now there's a tight angry
bitter knot of hatred there instead.

What is my supplication?
Stupid people and new mothers,
leave me alone.
Deliver me, Lord
of this bitter afterbirth.
Open my heart
to my husband-lover-friend
that we may comfort each other.
Open my womb that it may yet bear living fruit.

MERLE FELD

Over time, our anger abates, but our sadness remains, each of us sorrowing in our own way. Some of us mourn the child who will never be and will forever include that one in our family's story. Some of us mourn the loss of a dream, or the feelings of motherhood, or the experience of being pregnant, a vision of ourselves as full, healthy beings. If we believe that this birth was not meant to be, that this miscarriage was nature's healthy, albeit brutal, way of cleansing something that was not right, then we may feel something akin to awe, and a bit of gratitude that it happened now and not later. And we may be humbled at the mystery of life and the role we play in it. So, without joy, but with hard-earned wisdom, we may recite: "This too is the doing of God; it is awesome in our eyes." (Ps. 118:23)

Silent Rituals

Sometimes, words fail us. Sometimes, neither our own nor another's can capture the truth. Words, after all, are always exterior, garments in which we clothe our thoughts and our feelings to vivify them. But at times of great distress words can be too small, too tailored, too tight. At such times, we crave the loose cloth of wordlessness. We may seek the company of nature, of losing ourselves in the songs of the earth. We may seek the comfort of movement, of our bodies in motion. And with good reason. Even as our bodies brought us to this place of pain, our bodies can lead the way out. They move, and in moving, exclaim, purge, renew, create.

Instinctively, some women have turned to movement as the beginning of their journey to healing. Potters throw clay; sculptors sculpt; dancers dance. If you have a favorite medium of expression, explore it. Words are not the only way to pray.

Below are two wordless rituals. One involves planting, the other baking. Both embody the images of loss, desire, hope, expectation, growth, and luck.

Planting after a miscarriage

It was late spring when Fran Snyder Voremberg lost her pregnancy. A blighted ovum, the doctor said. Comfortable with being a mother of two, Fran was surprised at the depth of her feelings. She had suffered a miscarriage after her first child but had approached that loss as "a minor medical misery." This time, however, weeks went by and the heaviness of the loss would not lift. When she told this to her friend, Hollace M. Beer, Hollace suggested that Fran plant a garden and allow the natural life span of the plants to mark a grieving period—what Fran called a seasonal *yahrzeit*, "a summer-zeit."

As Fran tells it: "It made sense to dig in order to sow rather than to bury. What was there to bury? Hidden desires? Unfulfilled wishes? Marital resentments?"

She decided to plant a memorial garden. She chose a vibrant-colored annual to represent the pregnancy she had lost and two perennials she was not familiar with to represent the children she had ("because my two children—may they flower perennially—grow in surprising and mysterious ways"). She returned home, planted her flowers, and encircled them with large stones.

"I did not speak a word; I felt free of explanation and articulation, of ritual need or solace. The annual was a velvety ruby-cascade petunia, with showy bell-shaped blooms that proliferate on the ground. Planting has its own syntax: cleaning, arranging, digging, sowing, watering, waiting. I broke two nails, I stained my clothes, I sweated a lot. I worked alone. Friends visited; someone brought me water. When I had finished, my husband came to look.

The petunia flourished, rain or drought, until the cold, having shriveled it to a crepey wine-colored pod, gave way to frost, which killed it. This was the time, from planting to dying, in which I was to grieve and stop grieving. In fact, the grieving abated as I planted, and the inevitable end seemed, when it came, a natural part of life."

> In the warmth of spring, select an area of your yard or balcony or favorite window, and prepare the ground or planters to receive the flowering plants. When all is ready, make your pilgrimage to a plant shop or greenhouse and buy one flowering annual, for the pregnancy that was lost, and one perennial for each other member of the family. Plant these flowers in your garden. Throughout the summer, may they comfort you with their blossoms. A photograph of this memorial garden in bloom may be a healing keepsake in the cold of winter.
>
> If you miscarry in the winter and wish to plant before the ground warms up, start your flowers in a planter in the house and then move them outside in the spring.

Some variations

Plant a perennial for the lost pregnancy as well, so that the dreams that accompanied that pregnancy will be part of the family forever. Rabbi Karen Gluckstern-Reiss suggests planting an aloe plant, a tree of healing. After the plant roots, you can break off a leaf of the plant and dab the aloe that flows from it into your palm and the palm of your spouse, saying to each other, "May you be a spring that soothes the thirst of gardens, and a gathering of the waters of life." (Based on Song of Songs 4:15)

When the planting is done and the tools washed and put away, some women may choose to recite the following with their husbands:

> We turn the earth and plant the seeds;
> We wait for sun warmth and soaking rains
> To nurture our labors and send down roots.
> So do we wait for the Eternal.
>
> For You have planted within us
> The need for wisdom;

WIN A $100 GIFT CERTIFICATE!

Fill in this card and mail it to us—
or fill it in online at

**jewishlights.com/
feedback.html**

—to be eligible for a
$100 gift certificate for
Jewish Lights books.

JEWISH LIGHTS PUBLISHING
SUNSET FARM OFFICES RTE 4
PO BOX 237
WOODSTOCK VT 05091-0237

Fill in this card and return it to us to be eligible for our quarterly drawing for a $100 gift certificate for Jewish Lights books.

We hope that you will enjoy this book and find it useful in enriching your life.

Book title: _____

Your comments: _____

How you learned of this book: _____

If purchased: Bookseller _____ City _____ State _____

Please send me a free JEWISH LIGHTS Publishing catalog. I am interested in: (check all that apply)

1. ❑ Spirituality
2. ❑ Mysticism/Kabbalah
3. ❑ Philosophy/Theology
4. ❑ History/Politics

5. ❑ Women's Interest
6. ❑ Environmental Interest
7. ❑ Healing/Recovery
8. ❑ Children's Books

9. ❑ Caregiving/Grieving
10. ❑ Ideas for Book Groups
11. ❑ Religious Education Resources
12. ❑ Interfaith Resources

Name (PRINT) _____

Street _____

City _____ State _____ Zip _____

E-MAIL (FOR SPECIAL OFFERS ONLY) _____

Please send a JEWISH LIGHTS Publishing catalog to my friend:

Name (PRINT) _____

Street _____

City _____ State _____ Zip _____

JEWISH LIGHTS PUBLISHING

Tel: (802) 457-4000 • Fax: (802) 457-4004

Available at better booksellers. Visit us online at www.jewishlights.com

You have planted within us
The need for love.

We fear for late spring freeze;
We fear for lack of rain.

We hover over our fields,
Praying to the Eternal.

You do not stifle our fears,
You call us to face them;
You do not indulge our longings,
But reassure us as we discover.

We tend our growing fields.
We trust in You as we work and worry;
We trust in Your goodness
As we send down our own roots.

Deep, deep, into the heart of the Eternal,
Who calls us to learn and to love;
Deep, deep, into our own hearts,
As we nourish our growing devotion.

DEBBIE PERLMAN

Reflections

Find or purchase a smooth stone that has a surface you can
write on. With an indelible marker, write a word or message
on the stone, and put the stone in your garden.

*The word or message I chose for my garden
stone is . . .*

I chose to write this because . . .

Baking

Below is a homemade ritual, created and recounted by Debra Nussbaum Cohen. It seeks healing through a woman's association with her grandmother, food, kneading, braiding, waiting, feeding—all connected through wordless action and dedicated to the sacred task of making Shabbat bread.

"Making challah is something like mothering—first you mix the ingredients and hope that the alchemy of honey, warm water, and yeast makes its fragrant and mysterious magic. Then you stir and shmush them together with a firm hand, but a sense of delicacy, too. Then you put the dough in a warm place, cover it with a soft cloth, and hope that your work pays off.

"I have loved making challah since I was pregnant with my oldest. But this time I made it as a way of healing from my miscarriage—a shockingly bloody and physically violent experience. I intended to go to the *mikveh* after my loss, but couldn't yet, since I was still spotting. I intended to recite the *gomel* prayer in synagogue, thanking God for seeing me through a dangerous time. But I wasn't ready yet to face my community knowing that I would be flooded with tears the moment I saw the friends with whom I so recently and joyfully shared the news that I was pregnant.

"I looked at new rituals that Jewish women had composed to mourn infertility and miscarriage, but none felt quite right—they were too public or too formal.

"My pregnancy ended toward the end of the first trimester because I had a blighted ovum, a term that sounds to me like the eleventh plague and felt like it too. There wasn't any possibility of producing a child. It was an accident of nature, a misstep, a mistake that took hold in my body and fooled it into thinking that it was pregnant long after the embryo ceased developing.

"Still, I was so sad. Engulfed in a huge lake of sadness. I wasn't depressed, and I wasn't grieving, exactly. I did not feel like I lost a child, or even the possibility of a child. No person could have come from this mis-mixed chromosomal cocktail. I lost my own hopes for this pregnancy, my own thrilling anticipation at having another miraculous child to love and take care of and enjoy. The pictures in my head of moving my son's art table upstairs to make room for a crib in the bedroom closest to ours were not to be realized. Not now, anyway, and I hated that.

"After seeing that none of the rituals I had found felt right, I sat back in the recliner I inherited from my grandmother, pulled over my lap an afghan that she had crocheted, and opened my mind to what I might do.

"It came to me immediately. Challah was the perfect thing.

"Creating challah is about nesting and expectation, about creating home for my family. It is an affirmative, joyous process, my most favorite bit of Jewish women's work, perhaps because of the mystery of the melding of yeast with honey, flour with water, that results in something so much more than the sum of its mundane parts. I also love it because it means that I have a rare window of time carved out of my hectic schedule that I devote to nothing besides taking care of my family. And so the next day, I stood at the counter in the home that we are so eager to fill with children, and rolled out dough.

"After mixing and punching down, punching down again, separating a small chunk and saying the prayer that sanctifies this ancient process, I rolled and braided. And when each perfect loaf sat, waiting to rise once more, on its baking sheet, I carpeted its top with sesame seeds.

"I noticed the funniest thing after the loaves had baked up nice and brown and I'd removed them from the oven—one of the loaves looked remarkably like the Venus of Willendorf, that ancient fertility symbol who is all heavy breasts and belly.

"You can be sure it was the Venus loaf that we dug into first the next Friday night, after my husband, my son, and I each put a hand on the challah and thanked the Creator for making us as blessed as we are."

Reflections

I bake because it helps me ...

When I am baking I tend to think about ...

The best memories I have of my mother / father / grandmother / grandfather baking are ...

The things I do to feel better are ...

I do these things because ...

Hold Me Now

A prayer of comfort for the woman after her miscarriage. It may be said before going to sleep during the first nights after the loss.

Hayotzer,
One who shapes,
Who formed us out of moistened clay,
Who rolled and pinched and sculpted the world,
hold me now.

You who enable wisps of seeds to grow,
Who partnered the life that grew inside me,
shelter me.

Life was gifted.
Life removed.

Hayotzer,
shape me a place where I can weep,
and mourn the loss,
and let the blackness inside
cry.

Help me say good-bye
to the child
who was growing within me,
to the dreams I bore,
to the love I held within for that budding soul,
plucked away.

Let my voice ring,
a mother's call,
wild to the universe,
And You,
stand by me,
stand at my side,
and watch my tears fall and touch the earth.
Hear my pain and
hold me.

Hayotzer,
You who shaped me
heal my body and my soul.
Mend my spirit.
Thread new life among my bones.

Hayotzer, one of seventy names of God, is translated roughly as "One who fashions, forms, creates."

Help me to find ground again.
To feel the earth beneath my toes.
To smell the beckoning scent of rich soil.
To see shoots of green emerge through winter beds,
determined hands grasping life.
To hear the sap rushing within.

I kneel to plant
A seed of life.
An act of faith.

Hayotzer,
Sower of life,
Take my hand and, for a time,
hold it tight.

VICKI HOLLANDER

Reflections

Draw an outline of your body. What do you see?

What I see is ...

Color or decorate this drawing of your body any way you wish.

Now I see ...

A prayer for comfort and hope
to be said at Shabbat candlelighting

After the loss, we are left with emptiness and longing. Friday nights can be opportunities for reflection and peace. As we light the Shabbat candles, we cross the threshold from time to eternity. This crossing is of great moment, when the portals of heaven are open wide to those who approach, especially those who approach with a broken heart. For generations, women have tarried over the candlelighting, adding to the requisite blessing their own prayers of thanks, concern, and hope. Whether you light candles every week or have never lit them before, you may want to light them this week and accompany the moment with the following prayer:

> Turn me toward the light.
> Uncover the choices that flourish
> When I relinquish my yesterdays.
>
> Turn me toward the light.
> Unveil the hopes that grow
> When I face my realities.
>
> Turn me toward today.
> Turn me to a vision of possibilities,
> That denies apprehensions.
>
> Turn me toward today.
> Turn me to this moment of extension,
> That opens old constrictions.
>
> Before me You place iridescence
> To soften brittle sorrows.
> Let me rest on the cushion of Your care,
> Comforted by Your regard.
>
> Beside me You heap soft pillows
> To ease ancient grief.
> Bolster my courage with Your kindness
> As You support my head.
>
> Stretch the stiff limbs of my confusion,
> And let me rise, renewed,
> To turn into Your light.

DEBBIE PERLMAN

To the baby I never had.
To the memory that I carry.

How silently and sweetly you snuck into my life, one still, almost motionless August afternoon. No tree dared rustle, no wing dared flap as God himself carried your fragile soul and nestled it within me. And I knew nothing of your heart harmonizing with my own, until I saw your pulsing little bean shape. So tiny, but so large. You overtook me and I surrendered myself to you, to understand you, to feel you, to sense you, to talk to you as you did to me. You told me when to eat, drink, wake, sleep, always gently, kindly. How you transported me into your secret little world of sensations, of feelings. How you felt or heard no one but me. How you softened me. How privileged I felt. How graced I was by your existence. How I loved you. O, how I loved you.

How I so wanted you to be well. How I wanted to hear "mommy," not just feel "mommy." How I prayed for your health. How I prayed for my own. How I cried. O, how I cried for you and how I cried for me.

How under unforgiving fluorescent lights all trace of you was wrenched from me. I mourned for you, mourned for me, trembled at the hollowness, the silences, the chasm, the profound emptiness, the crushing devastation within me. How I miss you. O, how I miss you.

But as God whisked you away, a tiny bit of your elegant and lovely soul draped a veil around my heart. And I thank you, for letting me touch motherhood, for uncomplicated, untainted joy, for choosing me to visit, however brief and fleeting.

How I loved you. O, how I loved you.

REBA CARMEL

Sing us a lullaby

A prayer for the husband and wife to say during the first month of the loss. The couple may light a fragrant candle, whose sweet scent may help renew and restore their spirits. It can serve as a reminder of the pillar of fire that accompanied the Israelites through their trying times in the desert and as a reminder of the spices that restore our spirits after we lose a bit of our more complete selves with the departure of Shabbat.

> Here we are, the two of us together. The two of us alone. We counted the days and measured the weeks that our child grew within. But no more.
>
> God, You knew our desires, for You once enjoyed them. You know the pain that follows.
>
> Our eyes longed to see the birth of our child, just as You once saw the birth of the world. Our arms yearned to cradle our new little one, just as You cradled Your people when You bore them to freedom. Our mouths longed to sing soft lullabies of love, just as You sang lullabies of love to Your children in the desert.
>
> Sing us a lullaby God, to fill our silence. Sing us a lullaby to soothe our fears and comfort our sadness.
>
> Source of healing, help us find healing among those who care for us, among our friends and loved ones who tend to us. And when the time is right, help us dare to choose life again.
>
> Blessed are You, God of compassion, whose compassion continually renews us.

Reflections

Pillows offer comfort in times of stress or sorrow.

Try creating your own pillow for crying, your own pillow for healing.

Cut pieces of fabric about 12 inches square from old clothes, color swatches, or new fabric bought just for this occasion. Mix and match the fabrics as you desire.

Sew the two panels together in a rectangle on the wrong side, leaving one side open.

Turn the fabric right-side out, stuff with fluff. Put a prayer or poem, memento or keepsake inside and sew up the fourth side.

The fabric I chose was...

Inside the pillow I placed ...

I chose this because ...

Loss

Twice even the Temple was destroyed—
the Temple, address of God,
focus of prayer,
seat of God's name,
God's presence,
God's power.

We loved the Temple.
We came rejoicing
and in sorrow.
We came in feasting
and in penitence,
on festivals
and Sabbaths and feast days
and no special days at all.
We brought our sacrifices
and our songs,
the fruits of our labors.

We loved the Temple
and the God whose Presence filled the Temple
and yet, the Temple was destroyed.

Was there something terribly wrong with the Temple?
Something that could not have been fixed
short of destruction?

There were worlds that God created and destroyed
before our world came to be.
What was wrong with them?
Was God practicing the art of creation
or whimsically testing the power to end?

Some are not meant to be.
Some disappear before they even arrive.
What was wrong now?
Is this destruction a mercy?

Or is it You, God—
Has Your right arm withered?
Have You lost Your power?
Is all Your great and glorious might
lost in the battles of the past?

Or is it only in battle that we find Your presence?
In the hearts of men,
and not in the wombs of women?

Yet I will recall the mighty deeds of God,
I will keep them before my eyes.
I recite them by day and by night.

TIKVA FRYMER-KENSKY

Living waters

After a miscarriage, after the bleeding stops, the woman may choose
to go to the mikveh to thank God for the powers of recovery and
renewal, to renew herself in the waters of creation. Or she may prepare for herself a luxurious bath full of bubbles and soaps and scents.
Just before she enters the water, she can say the following prayer:

> The parting of water is the start of all creation, as it says,
> "And God separated the waters above from the waters

below." (Gen. 1:7) Let these waters that for me now part be waters of life. Dear God, I stand here at the edge, aching for the child I could not hold. Let these waters that I enter now hold me. Let them flow over me and wash away my despair. Let them relieve me of my pain and renew in me the powers of life. God of all life, as I slip into these waters, let me know that I slip into Your loving hands.

A synagogue ritual

For families who seek comfort after a miscarriage within the circle of their congregation, the weekly Shabbat Torah service provides a sacred setting. It is during the Torah service that the rabbi chants the *mi shebeirakh*, the personal prayer for healing. It is during the Torah service that the congregation stands together to proclaim the coming of the new month and ask that it be one of blessing and happiness, life and strength. It is during the Torah service that the congregation recites the *Yizkor* prayers, remembering the lives and legacies of loved ones who have died. And it is during the Torah service that the person who has recovered from illness, returned from any overseas trip, or survived an accident or misfortune recites *birkat ha-gomel*, the blessing of thanks and deliverance.

Rabbi Susan Grossman wove together the following verses as part of an introduction to the recitation of *birkat ha-gomel* for one who suffered a miscarriage:

> "He blossoms like a flower and withers; he vanishes like a shadow and does not endure. . . . Seeing his days are determined, the number of his months are with You, You set him limits that he *could* not pass." (Job 14:2, 5)
>
> Oh God, I commend back to Your safekeeping the potential life entrusted to me for so short a time, even as I grieve its passing out of the protection of my body.
>
> "You know when the wild goats of the rock give birth, You mark when the hinds calve." (Job 39:1)

You created the miracle of birth and the wonder of the
body that cares for mother and child. *Dayyan Ha'emet*, Righteous
Judge, You care for Your creatures even when such care tastes
bitter. *Harachaman*, Merciful One, heal my body and soul; heal
my womb so that I may carry to term a healthy soul, that I may
come to sing Your praises as a happy mother surrounded by her
children in the courtyards of a Jerusalem at peace.

Blessed are You, Almighty God, Sovereign of the universe, who bestows kindness on the undeserving and has
shown me every kindness.

The congregation responds:

May the One who has shown you every kindness, ever show
kindness to you. Amen.

The rabbi may offer the following *mi shebeirakh*, a special prayer of
comfort and healing for the couple, composed by Rabbi Amy Eilberg:

May God who blessed our ancestors, Abraham, Isaac, and
Jacob, Sarah, Rebecca, Rachel and Leah, grant this family
refu'at hanefesh urefu'at haguf, a full healing of body and spirit,
abundant blessing from loved ones, and an awareness of God's
presence with them in their pain. As for the baby that was not
to be, shelter this spirit, O God, in the shadow of Your wings,
for You, God of parents, God of children, God of us all, guard
and shelter us. You are a gracious and loving God. Guard our
coming and our going, grant us life and peace, now and
always, for You are the Source of life and peace. May we as a
holy community support and love our friends in times of pain
as well as times of joy. And as we have wept together, so may
we soon gather to rejoice. Amen.

In response, the woman or couple may say:

God heals the broken-hearted.
  and binds up their wounds.
God reckons the number of stars,
  giving each one its name.

Great is God and full of power
   whose wisdom is beyond reckoning
God gives courage to the lowly
   and brings hope to those bereft.
So may God always be with us.

(BASED ON PS. 147:2–6)

Havdalah ritual after a miscarriage

Havdalah means separation, distinction, acknowledging the difference
between this moment and that, what has past and what is yet to be,
that status and this. It is also the name of the Saturday night ritual that
marks the crossing of the threshold from Shabbat to the rest of the
week. The symbols of closure, transition, and hope in the future that
naturally occur in *Havdalah* generously lend themselves to a ritual
marking the acceptance of one's loss. The following ceremony is
inspired by a *Havdalah* ritual developed by Rabbi Shira Stern.

Families and friends may be invited to participate. Foods for
the evening may consist of a round challah, hard-boiled eggs,
grapes, lentils, and other round foods. A braided candle, cup of
wine and spices will be used during the ritual.

With friends and family gathered around, the couple lights
the *Havdalah* candle. It may be held by the woman or passed
among the participants as they speak.

A participant begins by reciting the traditional opening
paragraph:

"Behold, God is our deliverance. I shall trust in God, and not
be afraid. The Eternal is our strength and song. God shall
always be with us as our protector, as it says, And you shall
draw waters in joy, from the springs of deliverance. It is God

who will deliver us; God's blessings are upon us. Selah. God is with us, the God of Jacob is our fortress. Happy is the one who trusts in God. God of salvation, You answer us whenever we call. And for the Jews there was light and joy, gladness and desire. So may it be for us. I lift the cup of deliverance, and call upon the name of God."

Participant (taking the candle):

When Shabbat begins, we light two or more candles. They stand side by side, as a pair, but each alone. When Shabbat ends, we also light two or more candles. But these are bound and wound around each other, joined by the spirit of oneness of Shabbat, casting their light together as one. Like them, we gather now, at the close of Shabbat, joining with you [name the ones who suffered the loss] at this moment of sadness. Through our love and our caring, now and for a hundred tomorrows, may you know the blessings of comfort and strength.

The couple steps forward, receives the candle, and recites:

Adonai, we are blessed by the presence of our loved ones tonight. You, too, be with us to mend our broken hopes. Give us the faith to turn to You in our times of hurt. Give us the desire to turn to each other in our times of sadness. Let the rays of light that flow from this candle weave themselves into a garment of hope for my husband/wife and me, and may we soon once again see joy in each other's one's eyes.

Participant:

"And Hannah arose after eating and drinking at Shiloh. She was desperately sad and prayed to God; and she cried and cried. Eli watched her mouth while Hannah prayed silently. Only her lips moved, but she did not make a sound. Eli thought her drunk and berated her: How long will you go on in this drunkenness? Remove the wine from your ways. But Hannah replied: Oh no, my lord, I have not drunk wine or any strong drink. I speak this way out of my anguish and distress. And Eli replied: Go in peace and may the God of Israel grant you what you have asked."

(If the couple hopes for another pregnancy, the following paragraph should be added. Participant:

> "Elkanah knew his wife Hannah, and God remembered Hannah, and she conceived, and at the turn of the year she bore a son. . . . When she weaned him, she took him up with her to Shiloh, along with meat, flour, and a jug of wine. . . .")

Participant raises the cup:

> This is Hannah's cup, which fortified her when she turned to God, beseeching the Eternal to give her a child. Drink from it as Hannah did, and we will say to you as Eli did to her: "May the God of Israel grant what you have asked."

(If the couple hopes for another pregnancy, the participant continues:

> May the time come when we may once again gather here with you, with food and flour and a jug of wine, to drink from Hannah's cup, filled to the brim with her words of joy.)

Couple receives the cup of grape juice, recites the blessing, and drinks.

> *Barukh ata adonai eloheinu melekh ha'olam, borei pri hagafen.*

> Blessed are You, God of all creation, who creates the fruit of the vine.

Participant holds up the spice container and says:

> On Shabbat, we are endowed with a second soul, a *neshamah yeteirah,* which leaves with the last light of Shabbat. To revive us as we endure this loss of soul, we smell the fragrance of at least two spices.
>   On this Saturday night, may these spices sustain you after the loss of the one you hoped and dreamed would be your additional soul.

The couple holds the spice box and recites:

> "Let God anoint us with the oil of gladness, and let myrrh and aloe and cassia be our garments." (Based on Ps. 45:9)

All recite blessing over the spices:

> *Barukh ata adonai eloheinu melekh ha'olam, borei minei b'samim.*

> Blessed are You, God of all, who creates a world full of spices.

Pass around the spice box for all to sniff.
Participant takes the candle and says:

> Light is the beginning of all life, for God's first words of creation were "Let there be light." "*Adonai* is my light and my help." (Ps. 27:1) "You are the source of all life; by Your light do we see light." (Ps. 36:10)

Couple takes the candle and says:

> "The Jews enjoyed light and happiness, joy and esteem; so may it be for us."

They recite the blessing over the light.

> *Barukh ata adonai eloheinu melekh ha'olam, borei m'orei ha-eish.*

> Blessed are You, God of all, who creates the light of the fire.

Everyone looks at the shadows cast by the glow of the candle.
Participant:

> Elijah the prophet is a symbol of hope amid despair; of God's presence in a wasteland; of tomorrow when we cannot see the end of today. Just as we invoke the presence of Elijah at every *brit milah* (ritual circumcision), so too tradition encourages us to invoke the name of Elijah at *Havdalah*. Through the stories of Elijah, we are led to believe that we, too, merit everyday miracles. We end this ceremony of *Havdalah* and healing by singing of Elijah.

> *Eliyahu hanavi; Eliyahu ha-Tishbi, Eliyahu Eliyahu Eliyahu Hagiladi. Bim'heira b'yameinu, yavo eleinu, im mashiach ben David, im mashiach ben David.*

> Let Elijah come soon, in our day, bringing the messiah, son of David, with him.

Reflections

The feelings of miscarriage can overwhelm us. We begin to contain them, corral them, tame them by writing about them. Once they are constrained by the boundaries of the page, so they may be contained in the wilds of our spirit.

When I miscarried I felt ...

The people I chose to tell were ...

I never expected ...

Renew Me Like the Moon:
Toward healing after miscarriage

"And to the moon God said, 'Be renewed as a crown of splendor for those borne from the womb, for they too will one day be renewed like you and praise their Creator.'"

(FROM THE PRAYERS FOR *KIDDUSH LEVANAH*)

When Lois Dubin suffered her second miscarriage in a period of six months, she responded by creating a lengthy ceremony of remembering, mourning, and healing. She and her husband, Benjamin Braude, expressed their pain, fears, and hopes in a personal service woven from the symbolic language of Jewish texts and rituals. Using the words of Bible and midrash, they told their tale through those of the matriarchs and the destruction of Zion, and enacted both anxiety and desire for hope through selected mourning rituals and *Kiddush Levanah*, sanctifying the moon.

The little-known ritual of *Kiddush Levanah* celebrates the growing light of the moon. Distinct from Rosh Chodesh, which marks the first day of the month, *Kiddush Levanah* takes place on a night between the third and fourteenth of the month, when the sky is clear, preferably in the company of ten adults, most often on Saturday night right after the closing Sabbath prayers.

Woman and the moon are a classic couple. Both live their lives in monthly cycles, filling and emptying. Our ancient rabbis taught that welcoming the moon in its time is like welcoming the face of the Shekhinah, the presence of God dwelling among us on earth, depicted by the mystics in feminine terms. Joining the mourning of pregnancy loss to the celebration of *Kiddush Levanah* places the grieving couple within the ongoing, never-ending rhythms of life and cycles of renewal. As the moon is with us in the darkness of night, so we pray that God will be with us in our moments of need. As the moon is renewed every month, so a woman prays for renewed fertility. And as the moon came to stand in Jewish tradition for the eternal renewal of the Jewish people despite moments of decline, so do the couple hope for the blessings of renewal in body and spirit after pregnancy loss. Through the creation and performance of their ritual, Lois and Ben discovered that the combination of pouring out grief, acknowledging fear, blessing the growing moon, and identifying with Jewish ancestors at a time of personal loss can help bring forth the first stirrings of comfort, hope, and renewal.

Lois' original ceremony contained seven sections: *Havdalah*, invocation, *Kiddush Levanah*, meditations and reflections (woven mostly from classic Jewish texts), transition to mourning rituals, modified mourning rituals such as reciting Mourner's Kaddish, and a ritual of closure.

Havdalah and the invocation help demarcate the moment as personal sacred time and the setting as a circle of personal sacred space for grieving and healing. Structurally, the invocation declares what is to happen and why; psychically, it summons the energies of the participants to overcome fear and enact the ceremony.

Below, Lois presents selections and adaptations of her larger ceremony.

Ceremony of Remembering, Mourning, and Healing after Miscarriage

INVOCATION

With stars shining in the sky and the moon clearly visible, the couple (and friends and family if desired) stand outside their home, or in a park or meadow. After reciting the *Havdalah* ceremony (found in most Shabbat prayer books), they recite:

> On this evening, we come together to bless the waxing of
>   the moon of this month of _____,
> to celebrate with the moon and the Shekhinah, and to
>   mourn our loss;
> to pray, to study, to reflect,
> to gain strength and hope;
> to prepare ourselves to make a new beginning.
>
> Listen to our voice, O God,
> May our words be fitting.
> Receive our prayers with love and compassion.
> Turn Your face of tenderness toward us as we turn our face
>   toward You.
> Return us to You and we shall return. Renew our days and
>   dreams as of old.

KIDDUSH LEVANAH

Praise the Lord from the heavens, praise the Lord from the heights, every creature praise God, sun and moon, heaven and earth.

Praised are You, our God, Provider and Protector of all the world, who with Your words created the vastness of the heavens, and with Your breath all the life within it. A time and a season You gave to them all, so that they not falter at their appointed task. They are happy and joyous to fulfill the desire of their Creator—the Worker of truth whose work is truth. And to the moon, God said: "Be renewed as a crown of splendor for those borne from the womb, for they too will one day be renewed like you and praise their Creator." Blessed are You, God, who renews the months.

May it be Your will, our God and God of our ancestors, to repair the imperfection of the moon, to replenish her so that she be diminished no more. Let her light glow like the sun's, let it stream with the primordial light of the first days of creation, as it was before her fading, as it says, "the two great lights."

WORDS OF MOURNING

A cry is heard in Ramah, lamentation and bitter weeping.
Rachel cries for her children.
She refuses to be comforted for her children, for they are
    not. (Jer. 31:15)

The joy of our hearts has ceased; our dance is turned into
    mourning. (Lam. 5:15)

Scarcely are they planted;
scarcely are they sown;
scarcely has their stock taken root in the earth.
God merely blows upon them and they wither;
and the storm wind takes them away as stubble. (Isa. 40:24)

Our losses press hard upon us, God.

The woman says:

Be gracious to me, O God, for I am sorely wounded. My eyes, my soul, and my womb are consumed with grief. I am like a broken vessel. (Ps. 31:10,13) Our cry, too, is heard in Ramah, with those who suffered before us and who suffer beside us. The cries of Sarah, Rebecca, Rachel, Leah, and

Hannah are echoed in mine, and in our lamentation and weeping.

The couple says:

Alas, how does she sit lonely,
Jerusalem,
once great with people,
Once full of life.
Bitterly she weeps in the night.
Her cheek wet with tears.
There is none to comfort her. (Adapted from Lam. 1:1–2)

O Zion, let tears run down like a river day and night,
Pour out your heart like water before God,
Lift up your hands toward God for the life of your young
  children. (Lam. 2:18–19)

We have no redeeming angel, just the two of us together,
  each of us alone. (Yehudah Amichai)

WORDS OF CONSOLATION

The man says:

And yet, our rabbis teach that on the day the Temple was destroyed, the redeemer was born.

The woman says:

And we know that every monthly menstrual flow is both end and beginning, a dying and an awakening anew for the possibility of life.

Every opening of the womb, timely or untimely, starts a new cycle on its course, a new personal calendar.

God brings everything to pass precisely at its time. (Based on Eccles. 3:11)

The couple says:

The Lord our God causes a woman to dwell barren in her house in order to make her the joyful mother of children. (Ps. 113:9)

God, it is said that You try only the righteous, as You
tried Sarah and Hannah, each according to her strength, to
dwell barren in her house . . . in order to make her rejoice the
more in her children. (Pesikta Rabbati 43:5)

We are not so righteous that we have the strength to suffer
so. Please, let the days of our testing be over.
Hear our pleas, comfort us in our hour of sadness.

All barren women everywhere in the world were remembered together with Sarah. All were with child and gave birth
to children at the same time she did. (Pesikta Rabbati 42:4)

After the weeping, singing will be heard:
"I shall rebuild Jerusalem as a joy, and her people as a
delight." (Isa. 65:18)

RITUALS OF CONSOLATION

The couple expresses mourning and consolation as they offer a
prayer for the one they lost (adapted from the classic mourner's
prayer *El Malei Rachamim* and based on Isa. 53:2):

God, filled with compassion, dwelling on high,
Grant perfect rest under the wings of the Shekhinah, among
    the holy and pure ones who shine brilliantly as the heavens,
To the soul of the little one, our little one,
the tiniest of beginnings—
a slight and small beginning,
a tiny and tender root—
lacking form and beauty and countenance
but still desired and loved.

To make the transition to a ceremonial meal, the couple washes
their faces and their hands. As they do so, they tell of Joseph, who
was overcome with emotion when he first saw his brother
Benjamin after several years:

"And he went into his room and cried there. And when he
was done, he washed his face and came out. Then, in control of
himself, he said: 'Now, let the meal begin.'" (Gen. 43:30–31)

All present join in eating the meal of foods symbolizing life, fertility, the Temple, and God's care: round challahs, hard-boiled eggs, and water. They may include other foods such as lentils, chickpeas, bagels, and grapes.

While gathered together for the meal, the participants may do what mourners often do in memory of loved ones: study a text from the Torah or offer a *devar torah*, a short, personal exposition of a classic text. They may also pledge a gift to charity.

CLOSURE

At the end of the meal, the guests take their leave by reciting to the couple:

> As the heavens are established forever, and the cycles of moons and of months are ever renewed, so, too, may your cycles of hope, fruitfulness, and love resume.

The couple says:

> May we, like them, become faithful and joyous workers, and our work truth.

All say:

> May the words of the psalmist come true:

> "Though they walk weeping while bearing their sacks of seed, they shall return with songs of joy, carrying their sheaves of grain." (Ps. 126:6)

LOIS DUBIN

A text that lends itself well to study here is from the ninth chapter of the talmudic tractate of Blessings: "If a person witnesses a shooting star, or an earthquake, or lightning, or thunder, he should say, 'Blessed are You whose power and might fill the world.' If a person happens upon mountains, or hills, or seas, or rivers, or deserts, he should say, 'Blessed is the One who fashions creation.' For rain and good tidings, one should say: 'Blessed are You, who is good and does good.' For bad tidings, one should say, 'Blessed are You, the true Judge.' If a person builds a house or buys new vessels, he should say, 'Blessed are You who has given us life.'"

Reflections

The moon in its constancy of change seems intimate and familiar, forgiving and reassuring. Conjure up an image of the moon or, better yet, go out one night and look at it again. And then write:

When I look at the moon, I see ...

This is how I am like the moon ...

Just as the moon has a light side, so do I ...

Just as the moon has a dark side, so do I ...

A Song of Love

A prayer to be said when the husband and wife once again lie with each other or when the woman visits the *mikveh* for the first time since the loss.

Eternal God, I thank You for the gift of love, the love You have shown me by sending me speedy healing. I thank You too for the love I find every day, the steadfast love and support I have received from [husband's name].

Once we stood beneath the canopy and heard these words: Thank You God, for creating joy and gladness, bride and groom, pleasure, song, delight and happiness, love and harmony, peace and companionship.

Tonight, as my body resumes the cycles You set for it, I prepare to return to my husband, so that we may together rediscover the joy and gladness, love and harmony, that is so important to us both.

Be with us tonight and for the rest of our lives. May we ever be mindful that You are the third partner that truly illumines our home. Help us to find not only joy and gladness, but peace as well. Help us to be worthy of the gift of love You have given us.

May my immersion wash away the pain of loss and grief, and may I emerge renewed and strengthened.

DIANE COHEN

Therapeutic loss

Sometimes, due either to the health of the mother or the malformation of the fetus, a wanted pregnancy must be ended therapeutically. Indeed, in Jewish law, sometimes there is no choice: the pregnancy must be terminated if it threatens the well-being of the mother. In such cases, the moment of loss is planned for and scheduled. We know we must say good-bye before we ever said hello.

Prayer to be said when preparing for the end of the pregnancy

Dear one of mine,

Imagine all the good that there would be, if I could let you grow inside of me . . .

You'd kick and turn, and make me bloom in ways I've never known.

I'd decorate your room and guess the color of your hair.

And when you were born, I would hold you and gaze at you in wonder, in awe. I would watch you fill your tiny clothes that filled my sweetest dreams.

I could see you stand on tiptoe, stretching bravely, hard as you might to reach the bathroom light. We could have cuddled as we read the books of childhood, and stormed castles with our sock-puppets and cardboard daggers.

We could have played hide-and-seek through the house, and hugged each other tight when thunder roared,

And I would have heard you laugh as you talked with friends behind your bedroom door.

If only I could let you grow inside of me . . .

But now, before we ever said hello, we must say good-bye.

O God, hold me through my hurt, through this most awful moment. Take that which was to have been my baby and clasp her/him close to You, forever. Be with her/him, God, and be with me.

A lullaby for courage

A new psalm for the woman to say when she goes to end her pregnancy or when labor begins.

O Eternal, hold me with gentleness
Through this long night of pain;
Lay Your cool hand upon my body.
As a mother strokes the fevered brow
Of her beloved child,
Give me succor.

O Eternal, clasp me to Your bosom,
And rock me with quiet motion,
To and fro as the seconds pass,
Waiting, waiting for the next relief,
Stretching endlessly toward the dawn.

O Eternal, sing me to calm,
Humming a lullaby my grandmother sang
As she arranged the soup bowl on the tray,
And brought it to me with the warmth of her smile.
Sing me that song to soothe my soul.

O Eternal, guard me through this darkness.
Wrap me in a soft, worn quilt of Your regard
That I might find a paragraph of flickering comfort
To read and remember
Within this long, grim novel.

O Eternal, keep me safe through this night;
And let the morning come to renew me,
To turn me, to heal me,
To find me enfolded in the vigor of Your love.

DEBBIE PERLMAN

Ritual for grief following therapeutic loss

As suggested by Rabbi Amy Eilberg, the couple begins by sitting on low, hard stools, reflecting the hard place in which they find themselves.

Rabbi or participant:

We had hoped to gather soon to celebrate with you the birth of your child. Instead we are here, joined in your sadness. In your womb, _____ [mother's name], was the stirring of life. This baby had begun to grow inside you, and so, too, in your dreams and hopes and longings. Now joy has been replaced by emptiness.

Couple:

Out of the depths I call to you, God. Hear me fully when I call.
    God is with me, I have no fear.
    I was hard pressed and about to fall. God came to my help. God, You are our strength and our courage. I thank You, God, for having heard me. God, be my deliverance.

Rabbi or participant:

It is the blessing and curse of being human that we have the capacity to make choices. Sometimes the choices are approached with joy and daring. Sometimes the choices are filled with pain. Nothing can make the choice to end a pregnancy easy, even knowing that we did what had to be done.

(If the fetus was not viable, say:

> The baby you were carrying could not be. No human hand caused this to happen; no human act could have enabled this baby to emerge in health and wholeness.)

> Still, in the shadow of such a choice, we feel small and limited and out of control.

The rabbi or friend offers a hand to the couple, inviting them to symbolically rise from their place of mourning. All present (except for the couple) form two even lines, about five feet apart, with the participants facing toward each other as is customary for Jews at moments of bereavement. The couple then passes slowly through the lines.

As the couple passes by, each participant says:

> May God comfort you along with all others who suffer pains of loss.

The rabbi or a friend offers the following prayer on behalf of all who have gathered or who have sent their prayers of comfort:

> May God, who blessed our ancestors Abraham, Isaac, and Jacob, Sarah, Rebecca, Leah, and Rachel, grant this family a full healing of body and spirit, abundant blessing from loved ones and awareness of God's loving presence. God, shelter within your wings the baby that was not to be. For You, God, are the protector of all of us, parents and children. Guard our coming and our going, grant us life, and children, and peace, for You are the source of life and peace. Hear our prayers, God, along with the prayers of all parents and children in Israel and around the world.

A meal symbolizing comfort and life, with round, soft foods like hard-boiled eggs, bagels, lentils, grapes, and the like can be served.

The couple may be given a glass of wine to share, just as they did at their wedding. Here, however, before making the blessing and drinking the wine, they can say together:

> God, just as you have blessed the vine, causing it to bring forth fragrant and pleasing fruit, so may you bless us.

For those unable to conceive

Some of us know we will never carry a child. Our bodies just cannot do it. We may have been born with some condition or suffered an illness, accident, or surgery that rendered us unable to bear a child. While earlier in our lives we may have swept this knowledge under our emotional rug, at some point it may force its way out, tripping us up, asking to be acknowledged, held, and brought into our identity in peace.

Whenever this time comes, you can mark it by selecting a candle that represents this moment of acceptance, this moment of healing. Choose the candle for its color, shape, and scent. One evening, on the far side of dusk, but while a hint of light is still visible in the sky, light the candle. Set it on one of your favorite dishes or stands.

Then say:

> Blessed is the One who spoke and the world was. Blessed is the One who does the work of creation. Blessed is the One who has compassion for all the earth. Blessed is the One who redeems and rescues. Blessed is the One who brings healing to those in need. Blessed is God.
>
> God, with a word the sunlight breaks forth, and with a word the darkness rolls in. You give us the rich bath of light for life and the cool, quiet cover of night for healing.

God, I seek to be Your partner in this ever-renewing, ever-changing, ever-healing world of life. Accept me as I am, God, and let me accept myself, too. Let me be at peace with my body, and let me find joy in the other ways I can join with You as a partner in building the wonders of creation.

Blessed are You, my God, who has in kindness and wisdom made me in Your image.

Let the candle burn throughout the night, until it burns itself out. In the morning, clean thoroughly the dish or stand on which the candle stood, and put it gently away.

Reflections

There are moments when the choices stop. We are called upon to let go, accept, and take stock. When that happens, it can help to record what we are feeling and what brought us to this place.

What I know is …

What I don't know is …

What I lost is …

What I didn't lose is …

Where I hope we are heading …

5

Helping God Help Us: Prayers for Medical Intervention

It takes three to create a child: a man, a woman,
and the Holy One of Blessing.

(KIDDUSHIN 30B)

After a while, we may begin to realize that we cannot do this on our own. Our doctors become our fourth partner. Something so private, so pleasurable, so easy, now moves into the cold, regimented realm of the clinic. Our joy becomes chore; our hopes are ringed with fear. How much can we take of this? How much will it cost? How long must we wait? Will it even work? The pursuit of a conception and securing the pregnancy structure our days. Nothing else matters half so much. We lose ourselves, and a bit of our loving, in our search for our baby.

Though husband and wife are in this together, they are not always equally involved. Therapies may first focus on one, then the other. Or on one and never the other. Different experiences may lead to differing responses, hopes, and expectations. Strain and tension may dominate their lovemaking. Or their sexual relations may have no bearing on conception. Guilt, blame, shame, fear, disappointment, the burden of time lost, and the amount of money spent may weigh heavy upon them. Two families must be gently tended during this difficult time: the one that is, and the one that is waiting to be.

A prayer for the wonder of our bodies

This prayer from the morning service expresses awe at the intricate workings of the human body. It may be recited before or after an examination or a procedure.

> Blessed are You, our God, Maker of all, who wisely formed the human body. You created it with openings here and vessels there. You know well that should even one of these stay opened, or one of those stay closed, we could not long survive. Blessed are You, Healer of all flesh, who makes the wonders of creation.

Prayers to be said before an examination

The following prayers may be said over and over, as often as you wish. With each repetition, they nestle themselves deeper into our souls, bypassing the hubbub of the mind, and joining us to the hundreds of thousands of Jews who recited them over the centuries when they, too, were in need. As our sounds merge with theirs, our prayers become one with their prayers, and we know we are not alone.

> I lift my eyes to the mountain.
> From where will my help come?
> My help comes from trusting God, the Maker of all I know.

My God will not let me stumble.
My God never sleeps.
Behold, the God of Israel never sleeps and never slumbers.
God is my guardian, the protector by my side.
The sun will not strike me by day; nor the moon by night.
God will protect me from all harm; God will guard my
    spirit.
God will watch my going out and my coming home, from
    now and forever.

(FROM PSALM 121)

God, answer me in this time of trouble;
God of Jacob, keep me safe in Your midst.
Send help to me from the holy place;
May Zion be my aid.
God, grant my one great desire; let this one dream come
    to be.
Then we will rejoice at Your victory,
And dance under the banner of Your greatness.
God, please, fill this, our heart's deepest longing.

(FROM PSALM 20)

Another prayer to be said before an examination

Merciful God, healer of the sick and broken-hearted,
    when Avimelekh sought the cause and cure for the barren-
    ness of his house,
    You heard his plea and showed him what had to be done
    and granted him children in return.

So, too, did You visit and bless Abraham and Sarah, Isaac
    and Rebecca,
    Jacob and Rachel and Leah,
    when they needed Your help.

Therefore, I turn to You God, and ask that You be with
    me now,
    as I seek answers to my quest for a child.

When the doctor proceeds with the exam,
   poking and prodding every corner of my body,
   filling me with cold instruments,
   I ask that You warm my soul.

Remind me of the warmth of my husband's touch.
   Remind me of his love for me.
   Restore to me my dignity;
   remove from me my shame.

As You revealed the answers to Avimelekh,
   reveal the answers to me, my husband, and my doctor,
   so that we may work together with Your help,
   to bring forth a child.

Amen.

MICHELLE GOLDSMITH

Verses to be recited in the waiting room or in the examining room

God is my light and my help, whom shall I fear? God is
   the stronghold of my life, of whom shall I be afraid?
   (Ps. 27:1)

God, You are my shelter; from the battle of distress You
   protect me. You surround me with Your comforting
   presence. (From Ps. 32:7)

El Shaddai, Nurturing God, cover me with Your wings. Let
   me find warmth and safety beneath the softness of Your
   embrace.

Hold me, Adonai. Keep me from all harm. Guard my
   coming and my going, now and forevermore. (From
   Ps. 121:7–8).

"As at the Creation of Eve"

When Adam woke and found the hole in his side,
did he feel violated?
Did he feel that God should have let him be conscious?

Did he want to participate
—at least by awareness—
in the creation of Eve?

Did he feel that he was now less than he had been before?
   missing a side, a rib
   or his dignity?
Or was the goal of companion
and the sight of Eve
enough to assuage his longing?

Supplication

Into the hands of other, I commend my body,
into the minds of others, I deliver my trust.
I remember my love and my desire.
May they consider my being,
may we all bring life.

TIKVA FRYMER-KENSKY

Prayers to be said before a procedure

Out of the depths we call you, Adonai.
Adonai, listen to our cry. (Ps. 130:1–2)

Adonai is our light and our help,
Whom shall we fear? (Ps. 27:1)

As a deer longs for flowing streams
We long for You, O God.

Our souls thirst for God, the living God.
Day and night tears are our nourishment.

How downcast our souls in despair.
Still we hope in God;

We will yet praise God,
Our ever present help, our God. (Ps. 42:2–4, 12)

You will yet turn out lament into dancing,
Our sackcloth to satin, our tears to joy. (Ps. 30:12)

We seek refuge in You, O God;
May we never be disappointed.

Into Your hands we entrust our spirits. (Ps. 31:2, 6)

Verses to be said upon insemination

"And God said: Let the waters swarm with all sorts of swarm-
ing things, that beat with the pulse of life. . . . And God
blessed them and said: Be fertile and grow and fill the waters
with life." (Gen. 1:20, 22)

"You shall be like a watered garden, like a spring whose
waters do not fail." (Isa. 58:11)

"Let justice flow like a mighty stream, and righteousness like
raging river." (Amos 5:24)

"God is bringing you to a good land, a land with streams and
springs and fountains issuing from the plain and hill." (Deut.
8:7) Amen. And so let it be for me.

Verses to be recited
upon arising from a procedure

Arise, arise, stand up, Jerusalem, for you have been
    nourished by the hand of the Lord . . .
Awake, awake, Zion, clothe yourself in your robes of
    strength
Put on the garments that tell of your glory. (Isa. 51:17; 52:1)
For it is I, truly I, who come to comfort you.

Prayers of love

During this time, when there are ups and downs, the couple must
remember to tend to their love, careful not to build a family of
three at the expense of the family of two. So every now and then

the couple should retreat to a spot of their own and tell the stories of who they are in the rest of their lives.

They may choose to set aside private time and read to each other from The Song of Songs:

She: Like an apple tree among trees of the forest
so is my beloved among the youth.
I delight to sit in his shade
and his fruit is sweet to my mouth.

He brought me to the banquet room
and his banner of love was over me.
Sustain me with cakes of raisins
refresh me with apples
for I am faint with love. (2:3–5)

He: You have captured my heart, my own, my bride,
You have captured my heart with one glance of your eyes
and with one strand of your necklace.
How sweet is your love, my own, my bride.
How much more delightful your love than wine . . .

Sweetness drops from your lips, O bride,
honey and milk are under your tongue.
And the scent of your robes is like the scent of
    Lebanon. (4:9–11)

A red stone

Even for the most desperately practical among us, words are not always enough to carry us through. When hope and faith begin to fade, we open ourselves to other methods of support. So, alongside the medical therapies, the rational explanations, and the classic prayers, we may reach for something more, like the red stone. The Talmud calls it *even tekumah*, a stone of assurance, a builder's stone. The stone was thought to promote fertility, provide protection from miscarriage, and assist in childbirth. Whether ruby, carnelian, eagle stone, or chalcedony, the stone was made into an amulet that gave the woman a tangible, tactile source of hope and comfort.

The color of the stone evokes the womb and the red, red waters that nourish it. Through sound association, it conjures up images of a child. For in Hebrew, "red" is *adom*, and "human" is *adam*. Ruby is also the stone in the breastplate of the High Priest that represents the tribe of Reuben, whose name itself offers hope, for it means "look, a child." And more, Reuben was the one who brought mandrakes to his mother, the plant that grows in the shape of a small human and is thought to arouse the powers of love and fertility. In some communities even today, Jewish women have amulets of red stones made for them. They carry them in special sacks or wear them as necklaces and rings.

Many women find comfort in these tangible expressions of their hopes and fears. The physicality of the stone allows them to touch what does not yet exist and to cradle in their palms the hope of their dreams. In some hasidic communities, a woman having difficulty conceiving may borrow such a stone from the rabbi's wife. The stone, then, is seen to possess its own blessings *and* the blessings of all the women who held it before her. When the woman is close to giving birth, she returns the stone, endowed with yet another story of success. The stone becomes the community's sacred archive and transmitter of hope.

Holding the red stone in her hands, the woman says:

Dear God, *El Shaddai*, my mothers took comfort in red stones, these smooth, cool symbols of their deep, dark wombs. My mothers recited Your names and the names of the angels You appointed to look after them. They wrote these names on the walls of their rooms and wore these names upon their breasts. Although I may not know Your names or the names of Your angels, with this stone of my mothers I reach out to You. In taking this stone I take up their faith. As I place this stone upon my heart, may You place my prayers upon Your heart, too. God, You answered the prayers of my mothers. Join my prayers to theirs and answer me. Let others say of me one day, Look, she has a child.

Prayer to be said while waiting

Like the Jews in Egypt waiting for the signal at midnight, so I await the first signs of life.

Like Moses, staff outstretched across the waters, so I await the stirrings of my sea.

Like my people at the foot of thundering Mt. Sinai, so I await the welcome, wondrous turbulence.

Like a woman searching for her lover, so I await a glimpse of my beloved child.

Reflections

The spirit is often aided by the physical. Holding, carrying, even looking at certain objects can help us get through difficult times. What things help you get through the hard times?

When I went to the doctor's office I took with me ...

The things that comfort me are ...

They were given to me by ...

I found them or bought them at ...

Jewelry can serve as a symbol of love and hope. What piece of jewelry do you have, or could you buy or make, that can serve as your symbol of hope?

The jewelry I wear that comforts me is ...

6

Remembering Our Love: Prayers for Husband and Wife

Not every night is a time for conception. It could be the wrong time of month. You may already be pregnant or in the midst of treatment. It may be that your child will not start this way. Let these nights, then, become like the nights of simpler times, when you loved innocently, like the first man and first woman, discovering the secret pleasures found deep within each other's body. As it says in the blessings accompanying a wedding: "God, grant these lovers the purest of joy, just as You brought joy to Your first creations so long ago in Eden." Let these nights be for joy and love and discovery and passion.

Loneliness

Could I meet one who understood all . . .
Without word, without search,
Confession or lie,
Without asking why.

I would spread before him, like a white cloth,
The heart and the soul . . .
The filth and the gold.
Perceptive, he would understand.

And after I had plundered the heart,
When all had been emptied and given away,
I would feel neither anguish nor pain,
But would know how rich I became.

HANNAH SENESH

Seeking you

"In the innocence of my prayers and the purity of my thoughts; in my sweet meditations and my grand sufferings, my soul sought only one thing: knowing you, just you, you, you."

CHAIM NACHMAN BIALIK

Man and wife

. . . How good to lean my head against your breast,
The warp of sorrow and the woof of joy
To weave around your heart in peace and rest.

With me you are—who will my lot destroy?
With you I am—sleep on, beloved name.
I guard your altar, keep the sacred flame.

SHIN SHALOM

My lover and I

We have been through a lot, you and I. We have seen our dreams rise, and seen our hopes fall. Yet still we are here. And although we speak of three, we are blessed to be one. So despite all the tests and the proddings and the pokings, I will speak coaxingly, tenderly to you, and lead you through the wilderness to the garden. I will give myself to you in the orchards we find there, as did Yocheved and Amram, and the eternal lovers in the Bible.

There we shall respond as our days of yore.
And we will once again say:
I betroth you to me forever.
I betroth you to me in righteousness and justice
with goodness and mercy
I betroth you to me in faithfulness

and we shall once more be one.

(BASED ON HOSEA 2)

A wife's prayer for a husband's love— to be said over candlelighting

God of all, beloved of the people Israel, may it be Your will that You hear my prayer. Even as You delight in the love of Your people, so I delight in the love of my husband. As the days go by, protect our love. Let him continue to love me with a perfect love. May we know the sweet blessings of peace, love and devotion, tenderness and harmony, and deep companionship. Every day, every hour, every moment, let us know the pleasure and contentment of joining our lives, one to the other. And let us always declare to each other as You did to the people Israel: "I betroth you forever; I betroth you with righteousness and justice; goodness and mercy; I betroth you in faithfulness." (Hosea 2:21–22) I shall ever be yours.

Some nights are for rest, whether through medical direction or inclination. Let these nights, then, be for quiet and tenderness, for the presence of each other, and for the comfort of now.

Reflections

The things I love about my husband are ...

The things I love about my wife are ...

The things I love about us are ...

7

Pregnancy

Pregnancy in the midst of struggling against infertility is a complicated affair. The miracle that is happening inside us has changed our status but not our sense of self. We still imagine ourselves infertile, but with a grateful, insecure reprieve. Through the miracle of technology, or luck, we have been able to hold the promise of life. How long will it last? It has entered our bodies. Do we dare let it enter our hearts? Unlike other women who have had easier times in childbearing, we may view our pregnancy as a medical condition more than an act of nature. We may see ourselves more as patients than as expectant mothers. Slowly, with success, these images will change. But not yet. We wait to feel victorious.

Still, when, and if, our bellies continue to grow, our resistance to celebrating the moment weakens. Joy begins to show its face. Our lips soften and make the traces of a smile as we gently touch our stomachs and know that, for now, a miracle is happening there. We begin to open ourselves to the promise of life that is in us. We dare to allow the awareness that even in these earliest stages of pregnancy, our child has made us a mother. That is a gift the child gives us forever. And in return we give the gift of our love, in the songs that we sing to our bellies, the plans that we make for "us."

"Do not fear to love me because I may leave you," the little one calls to us. "I am here, now. That is all we can ever promise each other. Love me now."

Upon becoming pregnant

Rachel

I will sit here very still
till I am sure
this life in me is not my life
this pulse my pulse.
I will not tell a soul
until I'm sure.

When big bellied Leah calls me a dry well
I'll weep as usual and take to my tent.
Jacob runs from family squabbles;
he'll keep his distance for a while.

But when he says, "Enough of brooding here alone;
come out to the field again, love,"
I'll place his hand under my heart
to feel the generations,
and he will tell me I'm like Grandma Sarah,
a late bloomer—but special.

BARBARA HOLENDER

Prayer for a couple
upon learning of their pregnancy

One evening soon after learning of their pregnancy, the couple sets aside a quiet time to speak their words of surprise, gratitude, caution, fear, and hope.

Thank you, God, for this gift of hope, this promise of life. Be with us as our journey continues.

In the psalms we read: God establishes the childless woman as a joyous mother of children. Hallelujah. (Ps. 113:9)

Let this be true for us.

In the psalms we sing: Those who sow their seeds in sadness, will reap their harvest in joy; and though they walk with tears while bearing their sacks of seed, they will return joyous, carrying their sheaves of grain. (Ps. 126:5–6)

Let this be true for us.

In the Torah we recite: Your land will be blessed by God, watered from the dew of heaven and the deep that lies below. You will have the choicest of fruits ripened in the sun and a sweet harvest nourished by the moons. (Deut. 33:13–14)

Let this be true for us.

We turn to You, God, in faith and trust.

Blessed are You, God of all creation, for bringing us to this moment, and graciously bestowing favor on the undeserving. Shower Your kindness on us, and our child, now and for all time.

Reflections

After all this time,

I feel ...

I fear ...

I want ...

I am grateful for ...

Prayers to be said throughout the pregnancy

A candlelighting ritual

On the first Friday night after learning of the woman's pregnancy, when setting out the Shabbat candles, the couple sets out one more candle than usual, this one being somewhat smaller, signifying the life that is growing inside her. They light their candles, but not the new one, and recite the traditional blessing:

> Blessed are You, Creator of all, who has sanctified us with Your commandments and commanded us to light the Sabbath lights.

Then they say together:

> *Adonai*, You are arrayed in glory and majesty
> You have filled our world with hope.
> Our home is aglow in the radiance of Your divine light.
> *El Harachaman*, God of graciousness, continue to be gracious
>   unto us.
> Allow this promise of life to grow in me/my wife.
> Even as You blessed our mothers and fathers, Sarah,
>   Rebecca, Leah, Rachel, and Hannah, Abraham, Isaac,
>   and Jacob, so may You bless us.
> Grant us the joy of bringing forth this child when the time
>   is right, quickly,
> whole, and without undue travail.
> May the tiny one who grows within me/my wife be blessed
>   with health and happiness,
> And may the face of our child one day illumine our world.

Every Friday night of the pregnancy thereafter, the couple can recite this prayer, thanking God for one more week. Each Shabbat, the couple can count the number of weeks of the pregnancy, saying: "This is the _____ week of our pregnancy," much like Jews count the days of anticipation stretching the fifty days from

Passover (the beginning of redemption) to Shavuot (the longed-for Revelation).

The newest candle stands, unlit, as a sentry throughout the pregnancy. If this pregnancy is successful, this candle should be lit the first Friday night the baby is home, next to the candles signifying the other members of the household.

Should the pregnancy not come to term, the candle should be moved away from the Shabbat candles and lit during a week-night, sometime shortly after the loss. It may be lit in silence and allowed to burn itself out, reminiscent of the candles we light in memory of a loved one we lost. A selection of the prayers found in chapter 8 may then be recited.

Prayer to be said every day of the pregnancy

In the 1700s, the Jewish women of Italy possessed a rich array of prayers to be said at various times throughout the course of their pregnancies. They turned to God with prayers to become pregnant, to stay pregnant, and to deliver quickly, well and whole. Below is one prayer they recited throughout the nine months, seeking the continual assistance of God.

> *El Malei Rachamim,* God who is full of mercy like a woman who is filled with child, I turn to You with hope.
>
> With modesty and humility, yet courage of heart, I approach to place my request before You: Even as You heeded the cries of my ancestors: Sarah, Rebecca, Rachel, and Leah; even as you listened to the voices of the righteous women throughout the ages, so may you listen to my request. Send an angel to care for me and watch over me throughout this pregnancy.
>
> *El Rachum v'chanun,* gracious and merciful God, be good to me and protect me from all harm and disease, illness and hurt, evil thoughts, self-defeating acts, temptations of fear and despair.

Let the child I carry in me not be malformed. Give my child a luminous soul, a loving gift from Your sacred treasure-trove.

Heed my prayer, which comes from the very depths of my soul. Let my words reach up to You, God, touching You as Your love touches me, so that my child will be good, honest, and just, and able to stand before You and all humanity with wisdom, kindness, and dignity.

Strengthen me and make me hardy so that I will not miscarry. May the hour of birth be swift. May the child I bring forth have a healthy body, with firm limbs, strong muscles, and fine organs.

And send Your help from the holy place to protect me and my child. Spare me as you spare all the righteous women who did not share in the punishment of Eve.

May the words of my mouth and the meditations of my heart by acceptable to You, my Rock and my Deliverer.

Additional classic prayers to be said throughout the pregnancy

A prayer for a woman to say so that she not miscarry

May it be Your will, our God and God of our ancestors, that You be merciful and gracious to all pregnant women of the House of Israel, including Your devoted one, [her own name], that not one of them miscarry the fruit of her womb. Seal in, close tight, and stop up the mouth of my womb with the double stamp of Your holy name *Shaddai*. Let it not open until it is time . . . Let my womb be sealed with Your two holy seals, one nestled inside the other. Let them be like the verses that say, "A locked garden is my sister, my bride; a spring sealed up; a fountain secure . . . Your children within you shall be blessed . . . There shall be no barren or childless parent in your land. I will bring to their fullness your number of days." Ease the days of all who are pregnant and make their labor short and productive . . . Give them and the fruit in their wombs life from the world above . . . As for me, may my child be born at a welcome time and grow in health and wholeness. So may it be Your will.

Another prayer for a woman that she not miscarry

I beseech You, dear God, *El Shaddai,* accept my prayer for motherhood, just as You accepted the prayer of the priestess Hannah when she asked You for a son. May her merit assist me, so that I may be able to bear to full term this child that I carry in my womb. Look kindly upon us. May I come to know the blessing of bringing this child forth, in fullness of health. And may this little one grow to serve You with love.

A prayer for the husband to say when his wife is pregnant

Master of the World, I thank You for Your kindness, for helping my wife become pregnant with our child. May the name of the Lord be blessed and exalted above all blessings and praise.

God, may it be Your will to show kindness to all pregnant women and ease the discomforts of their pregnancies. Protect them so that none of them miscarries. Guard all who are in the throes of labor, so that no harm comes to them and that they give birth to life. Include among them my wife [her name]. Ease her pain; lighten her burden; let her complete the months of pregnancy and give birth with ease. Let no mar or blemish or illness come upon my wife or the child. Let our little one be fully formed with all physical and mental capacities . . . *El Harachaman,* God of mercy, deal with us mercifully, and not according to the laws of strict justice. Overlook our weaknesses and misdeeds, and act toward us with kindness and graciousness. Give us long life, and let my wife and me grow old together, proud of our children, watching them do Your will.

M'ugelet

In preparation for this ceremony celebrating the beginning of a pregnancy, a friend of Rabbi Jane Litman brought back from Israel a red cord that had been wrapped around Rachel's Tomb. Rachel is the matriarch who suffered years of infertility. After great difficulty, she bore two children, Joseph and Benjamin, but died from the complications of delivering Benjamin. In the Jewish imagination, she became one of the premier advocates for Jews in need, especially for the Jewish nation in exile. From her place amidst the heavens, she wept over their wanderings and was constantly beseeching God for their full return. Why Rachel? Because, according to the Midrash, in her life she modeled the kind of dedication, understanding, forgiveness, and love she is now demanding of God. And because she alone of all the matriarchs and patriarchs is buried by the roadside, in exile, and not in the familial burial cave purchased by Abraham so long ago in the Land of Israel.

The story is this: In 586 B.C.E., Nebuchadnezzar ravaged Jerusalem and carried all the Jews off to exile in Babylonia. The prophets said it was because Israel had turned away from the one true God and lusted instead after false gods. In an effort to convince God to forgive her children and return them to their homeland, Rachel approached the Holy Throne and told her tale: "I learned of my father's plan to give my sister, Leah, in marriage to my beloved Jacob instead of me. At first, I sought to thwart the plan and devised with Jacob a signal whereby he would know if it was me under the veil. But when I saw my sister preparing for the wedding, compassion overwhelmed me. I taught her the signs so she could fool Jacob. And not only that, but I crawled under the wedding bed so that I could answer instead of her and Jacob would not recognize her from her voice. If I, a mere mortal, was able to muster such compassion when my beloved was with another, surely You, the Compassionate One, can show Your people compassion."

Immediately, God relented and promised, "For your sake Rachel, I will bring Israel back from exile."

"Let your voice weep no more," the prophets called to Rachel, "and dry the tears from your eyes. For there is reward for your labors, says the Lord . . . your children shall return to their land." (Jer. 31:15–17)

Over time, Rachel also became the prime intercessor for those who suffer infertility. Her tomb, near Bethlehem, has become a shrine for women seeking to bear children of their own. Jewish women from all over the world make pilgrimages to Rachel's Tomb, especially on Rosh Chodesh, the celebration of the new moon; Elul, the month before the High Holidays; and the fourteenth of Cheshvan, the reputed anniversary of Rachel's death. They come seeking comfort and protection, for help with their infertility and their difficult pregnancies. They wrap a cord around her tomb and then cut it into smaller pieces, which are in turn wrapped around the wrist or waist of the woman in need. The following ritual is built around this thread.

The pregnant woman gathers in the midst of a group of women friends that stands around her holding a red cord brought from the Tomb of Rachel. She then recites this prayer for herself:

> Merciful and gracious Creator, have compassion on your loving handmaiden, [her own name Bat/daughter of her mother's name], that she may give birth to her child safely and in good health. May the merit of our holy foremothers Sarah, Rebecca, Rachel, Leah, Bilhah, and Zilpah and the merit of our great leaders Miriam, Deborah, Hannah, and Judith sustain me through my time of danger. May You help me avoid unhealthy acts and stay far away from any drink, smoke, or food that might harm the precious life within me. May this

---

Bilhah and Zilpah were the maidservants of Rachel and Leah and the mothers of four of the twelve tribes of Israel: Dan and Naphtali, and Gad and Asher.

child be born through spacious straits, with room to spare. As You opened the Red Sea so that the children of Israel could pass through unharmed, please open me so that this child is born safely and without pain. May this little one grow to be a righteous person, always walking in the path of Torah and in the pursuit of *ma'asim tovim* [good deeds]. And may the Jewish people merit true redemption in this one's lifetime. Amen.

The women then help wrap the cord around the pregnant woman in the center, all the while heaping blessings upon her.

All then partake in the ceremonial meal laden with round foods.

Prayer to be said upon entering the seventh month

Lord our God and God of our ancestors, may it be Your will that I [woman's name] easily carry the welcome burden of my pregnancy. Continually grant me strength throughout these months so that neither the baby's health nor mine will fail. Save me from the judgment visited upon Eve, and at the time of birth, when the days of my pregnancy are complete, let me not be wracked by the pains of labor. Let the child be born speedily, and may I give birth easily, as naturally as a hen, without harm to me or my child . . . In Your hand God is the key to life and birth. This key is not given over to the hands of an angel. Deal graciously and kindly with me . . . Just as You answered our holy mothers, Sarah, Rebecca, Rachel, Leah, and Hannah, and all the righteous and pious women of Israel, so may You answer me.

To prepare themselves, and the powers that be, for their approaching labor, Italian Jewish women would recite a verse from Torah that speaks of deliverance, leaving, getting out, exiting. It would be recited three times, forward and backward, repeating over and over the theme of labor: get the baby out. Spoken to Pharaoh by Moses when he foretells of the Jews' exodus from Egypt, the verse symbolically rehearses the delivery of a child from the body of its mother. "Then shall they all come down to me and bow down to me and say: 'Get out, you and all the people that are with you,' and after that, I will go out. And he went out." (Exod. 11:8)

Prayer to be said upon entering the ninth month

I thank You God with all my heart that I have carried the full nine months and that up to now You have spared me from all afflictions that could harm a pregnant woman and her child. Your tenderness is unending. Again, I seek Your kindness. Be with me and support me when my child presses to be born. Keep me from distress. Let this child emerge from my body full of vigor and life. May my child not suffer any form of disfigurement or loss, or accident or harm. Fill my breasts with milk enough to nurse.

Send my child with plenty of blessings. Let this little one grow in prosperity and health. Bless our little one, and us, with years of life, full of love, peace, happiness, and learning. Let us build a house worthy of Your name. Hear me, O God, when I call to You. Be gracious to me and answer me. May the words of my mouth and the meditations of my heart be acceptable to You, my Rock and my Deliverer.

Petichah—opening the ark, opening the womb

When the woman enters her ninth month, she or her husband should be given the honor of opening the ark in the synagogue on Shabbat. Just as the ark opens with ease, allowing us to remove the Torah readily from its midst, so may the woman's womb open with ease, allowing us to remove the child readily from within her.

Reflections

Checking in. Write your feelings, your experiences, reports of your doctor's visits over the months of pregnancy here. Include what you could eat and what you couldn't eat; the weight you gained; your sleeping habits; your wardrobe; and more.

I discovered I was pregnant when ...

My reflections at four weeks are ...

My reflections at eight weeks are ...

My reflections at twelve weeks are ...

My reflections at sixteen weeks are ...

My reflections at twenty weeks are ...

My reflections at twenty-four weeks are ...

My reflections at twenty-eight weeks are ...

My reflections at thirty-two weeks are ...

My reflections at thirty-six weeks are ...

My reflections at forty weeks are ...

Prayers for a woman in labor

When a woman is in labor, those praying on her behalf can stand near a doorway, under the mezuzah, symbolic of the threshold that the child is pressing to pass through, and say:

"It is I, even I, who comforts you . . . ,
     I am the Lord your God, who stirred up the sea and the waves within it . . .
     I have put my words in your mouth, and covered you in the shadow of My hand.
     That I may plant the heavens and lay the foundations of the earth . . .

Hark, you watchman, they lift up the voice, together as one they sing, for they shall see, eye to eye, God returning to Zion. Break forth into song, sing together, you desolate places of Jerusalem, for God has comforted your people, and redeemed Jerusalem."

Prayer to be recited
on behalf of a woman in labor

Until the modern period, childbirth was a frightening and some-times life-threatening ordeal. Worries of pain and suffering were joined by concerns about survival. Jewish tradition, therefore, cre-ated many prayers to be said on behalf of women in labor. God, who holds the key to the womb and has kept it locked for nine months to preserve the pregnancy, is asked to open it now.

Gracious, awesome, and mighty God, who answers us in times of need, receive our prayers, and the prayers of all Your people Israel, kindly and willingly.
     God, You heard the cries of our mothers and remem-bered them.
     Remember, too, in the midst of all the prayers and peti-tions that come before You, this struggling woman [the

woman's name and the name of her mother], who strains and cries from the work of her labor. God, see her sorrow and her tears. May her prayers rise up before You. May You safeguard her health and her life.

Deliver her safely from her travail. Open her womb and let the child come forth—alive and whole, without any blemish or injury. Bring both mother and child through the narrow straits of birthing to the wide world of life, as You did when You led the people Israel through the Red Sea in safety.

God, You who hold the key to life, open wide for mother and child the gates of light and blessing; of joy and gladness; of good counsel and good life; of healing and forgiveness; of deep satisfaction and caring comfort; of help and *tzedakah*; of security and health.

May the One who answered Sarah in her sadness, answer her. May the One who answered Rebecca when she sought God, answer her. May the One who answered Rachel when she gave birth to Joseph, answer her. May the One who blessed Leah, bless her. May the One who remembers all those who struggle to conceive, carry, and bear a child, answer her. May the One who answered Hannah, answer her. Remove her from the punishment of Eve, and on behalf of all the caring women in the world, save her from all harm, and send her complete healing, this time and every time a woman struggles to give birth.

The rabbis of old offered women the hope of an easy birth by teaching them that not all women were partners in the punishment of Eve. While God condemned Eve to suffer pain in labor, the rabbis taught that the merit of the righteous women throughout the ages might relieve laboring women of this particular curse.

A prayer on behalf of
a woman having difficult labor

There are few injustices greater than a woman dying in childbirth. Our ancestors struggled with this tragedy no less than we, perhaps even more, for the dangers of birthing were magnified in their time. Through midrash they tried to make sense of this awfulness: at the moment of birth, they imagined, the laboring woman is judged for all her past deeds. Just as on Rosh Hashanah, the birthday of the world, the world is called before the divine court to receive divine judgment, so here, on this birthday, the woman is, too. And like all Jews on Days of Awe, this woman does not appear before God alone. She has her defenders and her prosecutors. It is the task of her friends, family, and attendants to become the woman's defenders, to beseech God to silence or ignore the Prosecuting Angel and pay heed only to the voices that speak on the laboring woman's behalf. Each person who prays for her, who gives *tzedakah*, or does other deeds of loving-kindness on her behalf strengthens the voice of the defense.

But even if this defense is not sufficient, we can ask God to see her tears and be moved to compassion; to spare her and her child, so they may yet live to do God's work.

When the woman is in hard labor, the husband or loved one tending the mother should pledge a gift of *tzedakah* in the amount equal to the woman's name, as calculated by the numerical equivalent of the letters of her Hebrew name. If her Hebrew name is not known, the calculation can be done with English letters, A being one, B being two, and so on.

> May it be Your will, God of the heavens and God of the earth, God of Abraham and Sarah, Isaac and Rebecca, Jacob, Leah and Rachel, Awesome God, Lord of Hosts, *Shaddai*, kind and loving Creator who answers us in times of trouble, receive our prayers and the prayers of all who need you. Receive, too, the

prayers of this laboring woman [her name] born of [her mother's name], wife of [her husband's name]. As she sits on the birthing bed, she yearns for her God to see her troubles and her tears, and answer her. Let her prayers find favor before You, for You heard and answered the prayers of the righteous women who were unable to have a child. You overturned their destiny and changed their course, so that these childless women were remembered with children of their own. Remember, too, this woman as she struggles to give birth; her eyes look solely to You, until You bring her into a spacious place and answer her. Do not prolong her labor; but open her womb without further pain or struggle. Forgive her misdeeds, subdue those who would speak against her, dismiss any evil counsel. Make her dreams come true. Let the child come out, for life, without blemish or harm, quickly and easily.

May the One who answered Sarah, answer her. May the One who answered Rachel when she gave birth to Joseph, answer her. May the One who remembered the barren ones and the pregnant ones, answer her. May the One who remembered Hannah when she bore Samuel, answer her. Spare her from the punishment of Eve, and send her a full healing, on behalf of all our worthy ancestors and this *tzedakah* that we pledge. As this redeems others from pain and misfortune, so let it redeem her from pain and misfortune. Spare her and her child from all sorrow and difficulty, soon, and speedily. Amen. Selah.

Prayer of thanks for a healthy delivery

"And Hannah returned to Shiloh and said: I am the woman who stood here a year ago praying to God. It was for this child that I prayed, and God has granted my request." (1 Sam. 1:26–27)

Just as You answered Hannah long ago, God, so You answered us. You saw us through the darkest hours and brought us to this time of light.

Thank you, God, for being with us, and for giving us this child of our dreams.

May it be Your will, God, God of our mothers and fathers, and God of our child, that You again act with graciousness and mercy for all those who seek the blessings of a child, and all women who suffer the pains of labor.

May the words of our mouths and the meditations of our hearts be acceptable to You, our Rock and our Deliverer.

Reflections

This is how I tell the story of my labor and delivery ...

Stillbirth and Death

*"A day-old son who dies is to his father and mother
like a full bridegroom."*

(NIDDAH 5:3)

Where do we find comfort after the death of a child? The memories are few and overwhelmingly sad. The debris of our dreams lies strewn about us, tripping us wherever we go. Justice, if ever such a thing exists in death, withers when a child dies. If the child had been sick or ill-formed, we can speak of divine compassion in limiting the family's suffering. But even this is a mere patch of comfort. Faced with such overwhelming loss, we seek more.

"What does God do in the heavenly realm? God sits and teaches the little children who have died." (Avodah Zara 3b)

For the rabbis, who were themselves no strangers to the loss of children, comfort was found in images of God as parent, teacher, and companion to the child. When the rabbis speak of the World to Come, and their own place in it, they often imagine an academy on high, with God as the teacher of Torah and themselves as eternal students. In the days of the World to Come, the rabbis say that the righteous will sit with crowns of light on their heads, basking in the radiance of God, who sits before them. So when the rabbis sought a vision of comfort over the loss of their children, when they imagined where these perfect little ones had gone, they imagined that the children now live eternally in the presence of God, the Parent of Parents and the Teacher of Teachers. Even more, the rabbis believed it was not they alone who were comforted by this vision; God was comforted as well.

To labor and struggle is the price we pay for a healthy child. We are carried through our pain by the driving desire to see and hold our tender, warm, squirming child. It is part of the deal: we allow our bodies to be stretched and pulled and pushed and torn. In return, we are blessed with a healthy child.

But sometimes, we know, something goes wrong. The cord? The heart? An infection? Sometimes we are alerted beforehand. Other times, it is a shock. Noise, pain, pushing, prodding, coaching, ordering, and then, silence. The activity ends. It is awesomely, awfully quiet.

It was not supposed to be this way.

The questions begin:

Why did it happen?

What do we do now?

Whom do we contact?

Who will help us?

How should we mourn?

First things: most hospitals today encourage the parents to hold their baby, to spend some quiet, private time together. Some nurses may even offer or be willing to take a picture of the baby for you. Many families appreciate this. Even couples who find this terribly painful at the time are often grateful for the memory afterward. It may be right for you.

But this is not for everybody, and you should not feel compelled to mourn this way. It is not the only way. If it does not feel right, let the nurses know it is not your way.

Next: you may want to call your rabbi or funeral home. They will be able to help you make important decisions about tending to the baby, to your needs, and to the burial arrangements. The appendix in the back of this book entitled "Laws and Practices Surrounding Stillbirth and Neonatal Loss" discusses what can, might, and should be done. It is also helpful to discuss this section with your rabbi.

A stillborn baby (generally a fetus of five gestational months or older) should be buried. A private graveside funeral is best. The burial may be slightly delayed to allow the mother to attend. Sometimes the family chooses to name the child, giving the child a way to be called in future retellings of the family history. This name is then spoken in the prayers of the funeral. Names of comfort and healing, like Menachem and Nechamah, or Raphael and Raphaelah, are often given, even if earlier in the pregnancy a name of a departed loved one had been chosen. That loved one's name is then often held, with the hope that one day another child will claim it.

Funeral for a stillborn

"A life blossoms like a flower and withers, it vanishes like a shadow and does not endure. . . . The length of our days are set; the number of our months are with You. You set limits that we cannot pass." (From Job 14:2, 5)

Dear God, we commend back to You this tiny life.

This family mourns the loss of the child for whom they

waited, for whom they dreamed. They grieve for what might have been, the hands they longed to hold, the face they longed to kiss. Their arms are empty; their hearts filled with sadness. We are confounded by the overwhelming mystery of death, by our inability to shape life to our wishes.

Accept into the warmth of Your eternal embrace this our child, who lived within our family's embrace all these months. [If the family wishes to name the child, add: And let him/her be remembered by the name _____ son/daughter of _____.] Hold him/her close beneath Your wing.

We may rail against heaven and be angry at the blind forces that ended so quickly the beginnings of our hopes. But You mourn and sigh with us, God. We weep together for the little one who might have been.

Let the parents' tears fall upon us. Let their sorrow break against us. Let our love and our deeds be a source of strength for them. In the presence of boundless grief, the poet said, "*Ein od tefillah bis'fatai*; I am empty of prayer." And yet we are full of tears. Accept these tears in place of our prayers. For the Midrash tells us that while all the other gates of heaven may close, the gates of tears are always open.

Dear God, we turn to You for comfort amidst the presence of each other. Heal _____ and _____ [the mother and father] and all members of their family who sorrow. Help us, their community, to sustain them and care for them, as they gather their lives together.

God has given, God has taken away. Blessed be the name of God.

Be with the mourners in their grief until hope breaks through like the dawn upon the night.

El Malei Rachamim, God filled with compassion, dwelling on high, grant perfect rest under the wings of the Shekhinah to the soul of this little one, our little one, [if the baby was given a name, add it here]. Place this tiniest of beginnings, a slight and small beginning, a tiny and tender root, lacking form and beauty and countenance, but still desired and loved, among the holy and pure ones who shine brilliantly as the heavens.

If the child was a twin

Sometimes a stillborn is survived by a twin who may be vigorous and healthy or weak and in need of great care. The feelings toward the surviving child are borne along with the grief over the child who died. They do not erase the loss or make it easier. To the contrary, for the moment, they make the loss more complicated. If the surviving child is in need of medical care, the family can offer a *mi shebeirakh*, a prayer of healing, on his or her behalf. If the child is healthy and strong, the parents may offer a prayer of thanksgiving for the blessing that is theirs. But they should always allow themselves the space to mourn, even as they tend to their gift of a surviving child.

Mourning in the synagogue

If the couple goes to the synagogue on the following Friday night, they might want to ask the rabbi to give them a moment to recite the following prayer:

> Dear God, Healer of the broken-hearted,
> we mourn today, we grieve for the one who could have
>   been.
> We mourn the one
> who never knew the secret kiss
> that comes with Your sacred breathing.
> *El Rachum v'Chanun*, God of mercy and graciousness,
> we have loved and lost.
> Ours is the grief of dreams turned to dust
> We pray that You have breath enough to regenerate our
>   hope.

And if their child was born alive, they should stand to recite the mourners Kaddish at the end of the service.

Remembering

A *Yizkor* prayer over infant death

Yizkor is a memorial prayer that is said five times a year: on Yom Kippur, Sukkot, Pesach, Shavuot, and on the anniversary of the death of our loved one. This prayer, composed by Rabbi Ira Stone, may be said at those times by the parents.

> May God remember our [son/daughter,
> child's name *ben/bat* parents' names],
> who has gone to eternal rest.
> Her/his life was but the briefest flickers of a flame,
> extinguished before it had time to shed its light on the
>   world
> but not before sharing its warmth with us.
> Through the months of his/her gestation
> We prepared to nurture and to love him/her.
> And for the time that he/she lived
> we gave to her/him everything we could.
> May the memory of the joy he/she brought to us
> in the short time that we were together
> strengthen us and may God count that joy
> as the weight of a life filled with such blessing,
> binding through that love and joy
> [child's name *ben/bat* parents' names]
> in the bonds of eternal life.
> For the gift of her/his life without transgression,
> we pledge to do acts of righteousness and *tzedakah*
> that she/he may merit eternal life
> and that we may find comfort in this world.

A Father's Lament

> You in there, in that wooden box,
>   can you hear me?
>   I want to talk to you.

Why did you have to die?
. . . I miss you.

I miss holding you and singing you your special song,
the one I dedicated to you when you were half an hour old
    and I held you to my chest.

I miss rocking your chair with my foot
in a vain attempt to calm you while I write.

Most of all, I miss each day the *you* who might have been:
    not another Deborah,
    not another Ben,
    but Michael . . .

I will never share, now, your pride in those first uncertain
    steps,
your joy when people finally understand what you are
    trying to say,
your pain when he who said he was a friend lets you down.

I will not laugh with you—I never even saw you smile . . .

I will not comfort you when you have skinned your knee,
nor hug you when you would rather be put down,
nor yell at you when you refuse, yet again, to go to bed.

There are a million other things,
you and I will never share.

DAVID MORAWETZ

Lament of a grandparent

Grandparents feel a double loss when a child dies. They grieve for
their own sense of loss, and they ache for the pain of their children. Still, all too often they have no time to tend to their own
sadness, for they are too busy tending to the needs of their children. They know this ache is not like the ones they were able to
kiss away when their children were little. It is not even like the

pain of a first love lost or a job that got away. All they can do is be there and stay there, and love their children through the pain.

> How do you comfort children upon the loss of their child? It is not the correct order of life. I will never forget this day as long as I breathe the air of this earth. On the yearly *yahrzeit* I relive the sorrow we felt as grandparents and the burden of pain and grief our children had to endure. I can never erase the picture of my carrying a small box the size of a picnic basket from the car to the graveside; of placing the casket into the ground and covering it with earth. Together with my son-in-law, wife, and a member of the Chevra Kaddisha, we buried our granddaughter.
>
> MEL ISAACS

Grandparents' prayer of loss

El Rachum v'Chanun, merciful and gentle God, bring blessings of comfort to our children. Let them find the strength they need in the arms of each other. Guide our steps so that we too may be a source of help. May joy and hope return to their home. Though they find themselves in days of sorrow, may they always place their trust in You. As it says: How downcast was my soul, how much did despair press down upon me. Yet I place my hope in God, my ever-present help, my God. (Ps. 42:12)

Friends

Most of our friends and family want to help us through our loss, but they do not always know how. You can help them. Ask someone you trust to be your operations manager. Let that person be the one who receives and returns your calls, bringing people up to date on the latest news. Have that person, or someone they designate, coordinate the delivery of meals to your house. If you have other children, let a friend arrange transportation, baby-sitters, sleepovers, and play dates. Allow your "manager" to serve as your shield until you are ready to face the world on your own again.

Your job—when dealing with death and shiva—is to mourn your loss. The job of your synagogue and your community is to take care of you.

You might find it helpful to make copies of the piece below to give your friends—both those who were a blessing to you, to thank them, and those who were not, to guide them.

> Some people give me advice:
> "You must have another.
> You must talk a lot about it.
> You can grow through this."
> I am angry.
> Some try to make it better:
> "It could have been worse.
> You must appreciate what you've got.
> Life goes on."
> I want to yell:
> "You are right, but that is for me to say."
> Some try desperately to avoid the subject:
> I feel disappointed, disconnected.
>
> Then there are those, the blessed ones,
> who say in so many ways the only thing I need to hear.
> "I am so sorry, David."
> "I am with you, David."
> The ones who, even five weeks later, ask gently, as if for the
>   first time:
> "How are you today?"
> "How are you doing now?"
> These bring tears to my eyes.
> These you could not buy with gold.
>
> DAVID MORAWETZ

Waters of healing

When the woman's bleeding stops, she may go to the *mikveh* or prepare a luxurious bath full of bubbles and soaps and scents. Just before she enters the water, she can say the prayers found on pages 31–33 and 91–92.

Reflections

Place a cut ribbon in your journal.

Write a note to your child. Dear _____,

This is what I think about death …

Decorate a box and put the memories of your pregnancy there: test results, prescription labels, calendar notes, the tangible history of your pregnancy and baby. This box can be kept or buried in your garden.

When I closed the lid of the box, I felt …

9

Finding Peace

Time moves on. Our best efforts do not yield a child. We can bear no more therapies. We begin to look for a clearing before us. At some point we take each other's hand and say, "It is time: time to move on; time to put this dream away and reach for another; time to move toward the next stage of our lives, taking our broken hearts and our cherished memories with us." And so we gather what we have and head for the clearing, and the journey that lies beyond. No one else can tell us when to move on. But when it is time, we know.

Moving on does not mean we become different people, or bury the heart that broke each month. Our dreams for a child are like the first tablets of the Ten Commandments. Moses descended the mountain with them, carefully carved and lovingly carried, but broke them in anger and despair when he saw the children of Israel worshiping the Golden Calf. What happened to these shards? The Midrash tells us that Moses picked them up, gathering them gently in his robes. When the Tabernacle was later built, it had a place for this broken set of stones as well as for the full second set. So the Jews traveled to the Promised Land with the two sets of tablets, side by side. Like our ancestors, we too travel through our lives with the pieces of our broken dreams next to our dreams that carry us forward.

"When a barren man leaves this world, he weeps and weeps. But God says to him: 'Why do you weep? Is it because you did not bring forth fruit in the world below? Behold, you have left behind fruit that is better than children.' And the man pauses, and answers him saying, 'Creator of All, what fruit have I left behind?' God answers, 'The fruit of Torah, as it says, the fruit of the righteous is a Living Tree.'"

We are taught that God knows of the overwhelming pain of our childlessness. Above all else, it is that aspect of life that the barren one mourns at the moment of death. So, when God receives the soul of this childless one, God approaches and speaks tenderly, offering words of comfort. "Do not weep, and do not count yourself childless. For your acts of study and kindness, pleasantness and caring have brought forth fruit. They, too, can be called your children."

This story shows how powerfully our tradition tries to comfort those without children. It shows us that in addition to our seed, our deeds form the legacy of our lives. The acts of goodness and creativity we leave behind are as precious as children, for they too bear fruit of their own kind. The prayers, readings, and rituals in this chapter help us accept the limitations and the blessings of our lives.

Words of comfort for a woman who cannot conceive

"A couple in which the wife is infertile should continue to enjoy loving relations, for the drops produced from their love are not wasted. God assigns to them heavenly angels who watch over them. Some time in the future, they will be given a body. And at the end of time, every child will recognize their parents."

Reflections

Having reached this crossroads, time may open up anew and energies are often turned to other endeavors. Our art, writing, work, research, philanthropy, volunteering, nieces, nephews, or even the old man down the street often become our "children."

I am directing renewed energy toward ...

I find joy and comfort in ...

The memories I want to keep are ...

The memories that will always hurt are ...

Some things I learned from all this are ...

I surprise myself when ...

Prayer of renewal for husband and wife

We have traveled far together, you and I. From the heights of
dreams, to the depths of despair, we soared and sailed and
sought together. We are tired and bruised. At times we tended more to the task of creating a child than to loving each
other. But now is the time for us to return to one another as
lovers. For I am yours and you are mine. Just as we traveled
this way together till now, so will we choose a new way
together.

It won't be easy. The bumps and turns of the old path
hurt, but they had become familiar to us. Now, we go in
uncharted terrain. There will be things to discover; things
to relearn. With patience, we can find the ways of joy in
them and set the rhythms that will guide our days. With tenderness, we can set fresh goals for ourselves and begin our
family again, anew.

Precious Gift

The story is told of a woman in Sidon who lived ten years
with her husband without bearing a child. Knowing that the
law required them to part from each other, the two came to
R. Shimon bar Yochai, who said to them: "By your lives, even
as you were married over food and drink, so must you part
over food and drink."

They followed his advice and, declaring the day a festal
day, prepared a great feast, during which the wife gave her
husband much to drink.

In his resulting good humor, he said to her, "My dear,
pick any desirable article you want in my home, and take it
with you when you return to your father's house."

What did she do? After he fell asleep, she beckoned to
her menservants and maidservants and said to them, "Pick
him up, couch and all, and carry him to my father's house."

At midnight he awoke from his sleep. The effects of the
wine had left him, and he asked her, "My dear, where am I?"

She replied, "You are in my father's house."
He: "But what am I doing here?"
She: "Did you not say to me, Pick any desirable object you like from my home and take it with you to your father's house? There is no object in the world that I care for more than you."

On accepting infertility

Kaddish for the end of biological fertility

Kaddish is a storied prayer. It punctuates all formal services, closing one grouping of prayers and opening another. It speaks of God's grandeur and our desire to proclaim it. It is recited when we end a session of Torah study and when we remember a life that has ended. It is only said in the company of ten or more. It is a prayer of boundaries and bindings. Recited in Aramaic, the vernacular of the culture in which it was crafted, it is the people's prayer.

In the version below, Rabbi Geela Rayzel Raphael expands each word of the Kaddish, entering it, fighting it, wrapping herself inside it for comfort. Sometimes her ruminations play off the meaning of the word; sometimes they echo the sounds of the letters. At a time when a space in her life is being closed and locked away, she opens the words of this prayer and creates new places to live.

Yitgadal—May God's name grow great:
I will never be a mommy again from my own belly.
I won't nurse or grow large.
I couldn't hold you in my womb and I won't hold you in my arms. You won't grow within me. I won't grow as much without you.

V'yitkadash—May God's name be made holy:
I won't be made holy by the process of conception, pregnancy, and birth.

I won't bring that spark of Divinity into the world through
my body.

Shmei raba—the great name:
My name will not be made great through my children. I
will not use my power to name.

*B'alma di'vra khirutei v'yamlikh malkhutei, b'chaiyeikhon
u'v'yomeikhon v'chayei d'khol beit yisrael ba'agalah u'vizman kariv
v'imru amen—May God complete the holy realm in your own
lifetime, in your days, and in the days of all the house of Israel,
quickly and soon, and let us say, Amen.*
In all my life and all my life with people, I never expected
this. As my days and life pass, I grieve over days of
waiting and hoping and praying for life.

*Y'hei shmei raba mevorakh l'olam ulalmei almaya—May God's great
name be blessed forever and ever.*
May Your name be blessed forever, even if I never name.

Yitbarakh—May God's name be blessed.
May You be blessed even if I haven't been blessed with a
child.

V'yishtabach—May it be praised
May Your name be praised even if I can't find the emotion
to praise from my darkness.

V'yitpa'ar—May it be glorified
May Your name be glorified, even if I am numb to Your
glory at this time.

V'yitromam—May it be raised
May You be raised, even if my belly will never rise again
with child.

V'yitnasei—May it be honored
May You be held in honor, even if I never hold a child in
my womb.

V'yit'hadar—May it be viewed with awe
May You be viewed with awe, even if I never experience the
awe of birth.

V'yit'aleh—May it be embellished
May You be embellished, even if I do not decorate a child's room.

V'yit'halal—May it be hallowed
May You be hallowed, even if I feel hollow.

Sh'mei d'kud'sha, brikh hu—The holy Name be blessed
May Your name be blessed as my soul cries.

L'ayla min kol birkhata v'shirata, tushb'chata v'nechemata da'amiran b'alma v'imru amen—May the blessed name of holiness be hailed, though it be higher than all blessings, songs, praises, and consolations that we utter in this world, and let us say, Amen.
May Your name be higher than all the blessings, songs, praises, and consolations that I can offer at this moment due to my grief.

Y'hei shlomo raba min shamaya v'chayim aleinu v'al kol yisrael v'imru amen—May there be abundant peace from heaven and good life, upon us and upon all Israel, and let us say, Amen.
May You rest peacefully with Your decision not to grant me a child, knowing I suffer so, and may I yet find peace of mind.

Oseh shalom bimromav, hu ya'aseh shalom aleinu v'al kol yisrael v'imru amen—May the One who makes peace in high places, make peace with us, for Israel and all the inhabitants of the earth, and let us say, Amen.
May You who make peace, find a way to help me make peace with this, so that I may walk in comfort with Israel, and all others who dwell on this earth. Help me find peace, and move on.

A ritual for accepting infertility

This is a rededication ritual that may be done in the home or in a rabbi's study. It may be performed by the couple alone or in the presence of others. It may done at *Havdalah*, at the end of Shabbat;

or on Rosh Chodesh, at the beginning of a new month. Begin with
a candle. On the table should be a cup of wine and a napkin.

The rabbi, friend, or family member begins:

> We are here to witness the rededication of this husband and
> wife. They have traveled far together, much in joy but some
> in sorrow. In their journey toward parenthood, they have dis-
> covered places they never expected to go, shared experi-
> ences they wished they'd never known. They stand here as
> one—their stories bound together, woven in a tale of tears
> and strength.
>
> The travels along this path are done.
>
> Now, for a moment, it is time to rest, in the shelter of
> each other, beneath the protective cover of God. As the poet
> Bialik says: "Draw me close, beneath your wing; as a mother,
> or sister, when I despair. Your lap is a refuge for my head; a
> nest for my rejected prayers."

Holding hands, the couple recites the following prayer:

> How wondrous is Your world, O God!
> It is bursting with Your creations.
> The sea is vast with creatures beyond number,
> the woods and mountains teem with life.
> Yet, it was not this way that we would build God's world.
> It was not this way that we would build our home.
> Still, God, You have blessed us.
> Your light has guided our steps.
> As we loosen our hold on the sorrow and dreams of the past
> so let them loosen their hold on us.
> Restore pure tenderness and love to our marriage, like that
>   of the first man and woman in Eden long ago.
> God, grant us release and bless us with healing
> Grant us release and bless us with peace.
> Let us give to the children of the world, as though they
>   were our own.
> May once again the sounds of joy and happiness, delight
>   and rejoicing be heard in this household of Israel.

Blessed are You, dear God, who creates joy between
husband and wife.

To recognize this new stage of marriage, the couple takes a drink
from the same cup of wine, as they did under their wedding
canopy. And to symbolize the letting go of their dream and the
renewal of their marriage, the couple may wrap a glass in the napkin, place it on the ground, and break it.

As their next act, the couple may choose to dedicate themselves to a charitable cause, like giving to a local scholarship fund,
a children's charity, or assisting other children in need. For tradition tells us that those who assist in the raising of another child
are considered as if they too are parents.

A *Tashlikh* ritual for accepting infertility

Bonnie and Lawrence Baron built a ritual of loss and new beginnings
upon the tradition of *Tashlikh,* the classic act of renewing ourselves
by symbolically discarding our sins, or in this case, our feelings
and emotions that hold us back and weigh us down. Below are
selections and adaptations from their ceremony. The ritual should
be held at the waterside, in an open field, or by some woods.

The couple opens the ceremony with the following words:

To everything there is a season: a time to embrace and a time
to stand back; a time to sow and a time to reap; a time to
laugh and a time to weep; a time to hold on and a time to
let go. Our time to sow has ended; our time to let go has
begun. Still, in the recesses of our minds there lingers the
thought: perhaps it would have worked next time. Perhaps
we should try once again. Therefore, we need to cast away
our regrets and "what ifs" like the sins we throw into the
water on Rosh Hashanah. Let this moment be the New Year
for us. To paraphrase the prophet Micah, "God will have
compassion on us. We will cast all our qualms and dim hopes
into the depths of the sea." (Mic. 7:19)

The couple then takes bread crumbs, or fallen seeds or nuts, or rocks and throws them into the water, or across the field, or into the woods.

After a moment, all those present may pick up nuts or stones to throw, too, and join their friends in ridding themselves of past dreams and unrealized expectations. Then, the gathering turns back to the couple and says:

> A pronouncement of the word of the Lord to Israel through Malachi: I have shown you love, said the Lord . . . and I will pour down blessings upon you. . . . And all the nations of the world shall account you happy." (Malachi 1:1–2, 3:10, 12)
> So may you find it, and so may it be God's will.

And the couple says:

Amen.

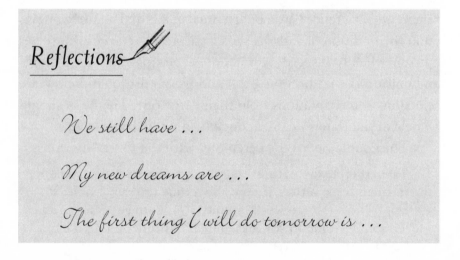

Reflections

We still have . . .

My new dreams are . . .

The first thing I will do tomorrow is . . .

Ritual for adoption

First, we seek to become biological mothers, the ones who become full with another human being, who birth a live child, who give that child food, body to body, who see reflected in the shape of nose and cheeks and eyes of the little one our own faces and the faces of our lovers.

But somewhere in the midst of our difficulties, when we fear that our dreams will never come true, we try to imagine ourselves another kind of mother, the adoptive mother, the one who becomes full with love, who gives a home to a child born of another.

Adoption is a difficult, sacred, anxious, joyful decision. It is right for some of us, but not for all of us. Friends and adoption agencies can help you think this option through. If you choose to adopt and the child is not Jewish, talk with your rabbi about conversion. Generally, the conversion rituals involve circumcision for a boy, immersion in a *mikveh* and a naming ceremony for both a boy and a girl.

Somewhere in the *brit milah* ceremony (for a boy) or covenant ceremony (for a girl), after the immersion, you may wish to do the following: The mother should be seated on a special chair. The father should lay their child on his wife's lap, nestled against her stomach. He should then take his place, standing next to her. A friend should be called forward who, while standing facing the mother, will turn the baby so its head is toward its mother's knees, and feet toward its mother's stomach. The friend will then slide the baby along the lap of the mother until it is entirely off her knees, and hold it for a moment. The mother will rise and join her husband. The baby will be given to a guest of honor. Then, the rabbi or friend will name the baby, saying:

For a boy:

> Our God and God of our ancestors Abraham, Isaac, and Jacob, protect this child, and help his mother and father raise him well. Let his name be called in Israel _____ son of _____ [father's name] and _____ [mother's name]. May his father be delighted with his offspring and his mother be overjoyed with her baby . . . Praise God, for God is good;

God's kindness endures forever. May this little child one day be great.

For a girl:

> May the One who blessed our ancestors Sarah, Rebecca, Rachel, and Leah, Miriam the prophetess, Deborah, Avigail, and Queen Esther, grace this child with good fortune and abundant blessings. And may her name be called among the daughters of Israel _____ daughter of _____ and _____. May she be raised in good health, peace, and tranquillity. Grant that her parents watch her grow in happiness, wisdom, and prosperity. May this little child one day be great.

All present respond:

> Just as this child has entered into the covenant, so may he/she be blessed with a life of study, marriage, and deeds of loving-kindness.

The parents then recite the following prayer:

> We have been blessed with the precious gift of this child. After so much waiting and wishing, we are filled with wonder and with gratitude as we call you our daughter/son. Our son/daughter, our child, you have grown to life apart from us, but now we hold you close to our hearts and cradle you in our arms with our love. We welcome you into the circle of our family and embrace you with the beauty of a rich tradition.
>
> We pledge ourselves to the creation of a Jewish home and to a life of compassion for others, hoping that you will grow to cherish and emulate these ideals.
>
> God of new beginnings, teach us to be mother and father, worthy of this sacred trust of life. May our daughter/son grow in health, strong in mind and kind in heart, a lover of Torah, a seeker of peace. Bless all of us together within your shelter of Shalom, peace, and grant our new family, always, the harmony and love we feel today.

Reflections

When I first held my child I . . .

What surprised me was . . .

My baby's room look like . . .

While I write this, I look around and I see . . .

EPILOGUE
Eve and Deborah: Of Mothers, Mamas, Mothering

There is still another way to be a mother, a way as old as the generations, rarely sung and hardly ever celebrated. It is, in Lorraine Johnson-Coleman's language, the way of being a mama. "In the African American community there aren't just mothers, there are also mamas. Mothers give birth to children and then love and raise them. Mamas on the other hand are women who love any child like it was her own:

> *The aunties, the sisters, the grannies and the nannies,*
> *the missus, the mamas, the madams and the mammies,*
> *the bloodmothers, the other mothers and the ones we called*
>   *ma'dear.*
> *All those ladies who lived in grace*
> *with their spitfire spirits and souls of sweet lace*
> *who could saunter down Decent Street, still swing their hips,*
> *dab a drop of vaseline, and shine their lips,*
> *and where they rouged their cheeks of sweet honey brown*
> *they shimmered like a rainbow 'cross a muddied ground.*
> *They never knew that they made all the difference in a cold*
>   *cruel world,*

with their hot-combed locks and paper-bag curls . . .
But Lord bless 'em and keep 'em, every last one of 'em
'cause without them where would we be?

They are the special ones you turn to when your own folks can't be there or won't listen; the ones with the backdoors always open; the ones who teach you gardening and patience; who hold tight to your secrets and believe in you just the same; who can say hard, true things you wouldn't take from anyone else. They can be anyone, and have any name. But, in their own way, they are all mamas.

The Bible, too, knows of mamas and mothering. Eve is the very first mother, *eim kol chai*, the mother of all life. She is the archetypal biological mother, the one who births children and cares for them, who clothes them and teaches them, puts them to bed, shares their pride, soothes their fears, and suffers their sorrows. But she is one woman, with one woman's strengths and one woman's limits, one woman's temper and one woman's ways. It takes that and more to raise a child.

Then there is Deborah. Early in the story of establishing our nation upon our land, the Book of Judges speaks of Deborah, the prophet/judge of Israel who united and strengthened loose bands of Israelite tribes as they navigated the course from nomads to citizens. She was called *eim b'yisrael*, a mother in Israel. She had no biological children (that we know of). The Jewish people were all her children. She gathered and counseled them; inspired, goaded, and guided them. She led them in song, led them in war, built them up, and brought them home. Because of her, we are told, "the land was tranquil for forty years." (Judg. 5:31) She might not have borne a child, but she birthed a nation.

Eve is the one who populated the world. Deborah is the one who built a nation. Both are ways of mothering that the world needs; both are ways our tradition holds dear. God holds the key to making us a "mother of life." But we each can earn the name "mother in Israel."

Reflections

We decided not to try anymore when ...

We marked the occasion by ...

We are dedicating our parenting
energies to ...

APPENDIX

Laws and Practices Surrounding
Stillbirth and Neonatal Loss

by Rabbi Stephanie Dickstein

This appendix is designed to help those who have lost a baby understand the Jewish ways of burial and mourning. It may also be helpful to hospital personnel and rabbis who care for families experiencing such loss. There is still much confusion, among professionals and laity alike, over what Judaism calls upon us to do when confronted with stillbirth and neonatal death.

Jewish law understands the death of an infant who drew a breath of air as something different from the death of an infant in utero (stillborn). Therefore, ritual practices for the two differ in some essential ways. Each will be discussed below. The one central element common to both, however, is that both the stillborn baby and the infant who dies after birth are to be buried in the sanctified ground of a Jewish cemetery.

Friends will tell you that Judaism does not countenance mourning for an infant that dies before its thirtieth day of life.

While this has been the prevailing custom, engaging in mourning rituals was never forbidden to these parents and in fact was expected in some places and times. Today, more and more rabbis are according infant death full funeral and mourning rites.

After the death of a baby, the parents should contact their rabbi. If they don't have a rabbi, they can ask to be put in touch with the hospital rabbi or local Jewish funeral home. These rabbis will meet with them and assist in making all necessary arrangements. Not all rabbis are familiar with issues surrounding early infant death. The parents should feel free to share this section with them, as well as to inform them of any questions, desires, or concerns they may have.

You may be asked or advised by your doctor to allow an autopsy. Jewish law is generally opposed to autopsies. However, if such a procedure could prove useful in decisions regarding future pregnancies, an autopsy could be sanctioned. Ask the doctor to do the minimum amount of exploration necessary.

Generally speaking, a fetus of five gestational months or more is to be buried in sacred ground. Most cemeteries have a section dedicated to the burial of infants and children. These graves are sometimes marked with stones, but often there is simply one large monument for the entire section. Minimally, the rabbi goes to the cemetery alone and buries the baby. Most often these days, however, the parents choose to be present and to hold a modest funeral service at the graveside. Such a service might be private, for family only, or it might include the members of the community who have been supportive of the mother and father.

The funeral home can provide you with a casket and a plot for the baby. If you have a family plot, the baby can be buried there. Some cemeteries will allow you to use part of a relative's plot. Others will insist on using a full plot. Before deciding where to bury the baby and what kind of plot to use, ask questions about where and whether you can put up markers, plant bushes or flowers, or use other adornments that are important to you.

Jewish funerals are held as soon after death as possible, ideally within twenty-four hours. However, a funeral may be postponed if a primary mourner is unable to attend within that period of time. The burial, therefore, may be scheduled for a time when the mother is fit enough to be at the cemetery. Usually, both parents prefer to be at the burial. As difficult as it is, it provides a way to say good-bye and begin the process of healing. It also gives the parents the comfort of knowing where their baby is, and it allows them a familiar place to visit in the future, should they so desire.

An infant born alive should be given the ritual of *taharah*, a sacred washing of the body. There is no *taharah* for a stillborn. Each infant is prepared for burial by being wrapped in a clean sheet or blanket.

There is no religious obligation to circumcise a son after death. However, it is the custom in some communities to do so while preparing the body for burial. No blessing is recited.

If the baby was not given a name prior to death, it is possible to do so during the funeral service. Naming the child offers him or her a distinct place in the family history. Often, the name that is chosen expresses the desire for comfort, such as Menachem for a boy or Nechamah for a girl, even if before the birth a name of a departed loved one had been chosen. That loved one's name is then often held, with the hope that one day another child will claim it.

The services and prayers found earlier in this book can serve as a guide to the baby's funeral. While the rabbi can prepare and conduct the funeral, the parents should share with the rabbi what they would like to hear or do at the service. Some details of the service will depend on whether the baby died in the womb or after birth. A service for a stillbirth will not include a formal eulogy (although words about the baby can still be spoken), and it may not include the full graveside Kaddish. The prayer for the soul of the dead may also be modified.

After the funeral, formal mourning begins. The rituals for mourning a stillborn and a neonate differ. When there is the death of a third-trimester infant born alive, all of the standard Jewish mourning practices apply. A meal of consolation is served upon the family's return from the cemetery. The family should observe the laws of shiva (staying at home for three to seven days, sitting on low chairs, men should not shave, mirrors should be covered, leather shoes should not be worn, the mother and father should not have sexual relations—a rabbi can assist you with a full understanding of the regulations). The core of shiva, however, is found in the visiting, by friends, family, and acquaintances. Anyone within the orbit of the mourning couple should feel that they would be welcome at the house of shiva. Since the mother is also recovering from the delivery, the hours of visiting may be limited to allow her to rest. Both mother and father, as well as any of the baby's siblings who have come of age, are mourners. Young siblings, if any, should be allowed to participate as much as the parents deem advisable.

While the grandparents are not official mourners, they too are grieving and can choose to participate in as much of the shiva restrictions as they desire. They can often be of particular help in caring for the other grandchildren, if they are so blessed.

After the period of shiva is over, the family may want to attend synagogue and recite the Kaddish for thirty days, as is the practice in mourning all first-degree relatives other than parents (for whom a child says Kaddish eleven months). During these first thirty days, mourners do not cut their hair, take part in festive celebrations, or attend concerts or events with live music.

At some point during the first year, the parents can arrange for a marker to be placed on the baby's grave. On the baby's *yahrzeit* (anniversary of a death), the parents can recite Kaddish, give *tzedakah*, and light a yahrzeit candle in memory of their baby, as is customary with other loved ones who have died.

If the baby was stillborn, or quite ill and premature and died soon after birth, the full rituals of shiva do not apply. A modified shiva may be observed for the first twenty-four hours following the burial, with the community coming to the family's home for evening and morning services. The parents may, however, choose to continue to restrict their own activities, and their participation in work and celebrations, and continue to follow some of the mourning rituals. Family and friends may continue to offer their help and support, but the family should attend services at the synagogue.

The parents may be guided by the following rule: "Anyone who chooses to be stringent on himself to mourn for someone for whom he is not obligated, is not prevented from doing so." (*Shulchan Arukh, Yoreh De'ah, Laws of Mourning*, 374:6)

The family should feel free to speak with the local rabbi for advice about any part of the mourning process.

PERMISSIONS

I gratefully acknowledge permission to use the following materials:

"Round," by Rachel Boimwall, translated by Gabriel Preil and Howard
Schwartz (translation copyright 1980), appeared in *Voices Within
the Ark: The Modern Jewish Poets*, edited by Howard Schwartz and
Anthony Rudolf. New York: Avon Books, 1980. Reprinted by
permission of Howard Schwartz.

"The Key," "Loss," and "As at the Creation of Eve," by Tikva Frymer-
Kensky, appeared in *Motherprayer: The Pregnant Woman's Spiritual
Companion*. New York: Riverhead Books, 1995. Reprinted by
permission of Putnam Berkley, a division of Penguin Putnam.

"Rahmana," by Penina Adelman, appeared in *The Reconstructionist*, April
1985. Reprinted by permission of the author.

"If I had a son," by Rahel Bluwstein, appeared in *The Plough Woman:
Memoirs of the Pioneer Women of Palestine*, edited by Rachel
Katznelson-Shazar, translated by Maurice Samuel. New York:
Herzl Press, 1975. Reprinted by permission of Herzl Press.

"Five," "Twenty-Four," "Sixty-Two," and "Eighty-Eight," by Debbie Perlman, appeared in *Flames to Heaven: New Psalms for Healing and Praise*. Wilmette, IL.: RAD Publishers, 1998. www.healingpsalm.com. Reprinted by permission of the author.

"Tapping the Stone," by Jane Schapiro, appeared in *Lilith: The Independent Jewish Feminist Magazine*, fall 1989. Reprinted by permission of the publisher. Lilith is published at 250 W. 57th St., New York, NY 10107; lilith@aol.com.

"Geshem," by Mark Frydenberg and Rabbi Simchah Roth. Reprinted by permission of the authors.

"The Bath," by Lynn E. Levin, first appeared in *The Reconstructionist*, spring 1993, and later, by permission, was included in the collection *A Few Questions About Paradise* (Bemidji, MN: Loonfeather Press, n.d.). Reprinted by permission of the author.

"Healing After a Miscarriage" will appear in *A Spiritual Life*, by Merle Feld (Albany: SUNY Press, 1999). Reprinted by permission of the author.

"Hold Me Now," by Vicki Hollander; "May God who blessed our ancestors," by Rabby Amy Eilberg; and "We have been blessed," by Rabbi Sandy Sasso, appeared in *Lifecycles, Jewish Women on Life Passages and Personal Milestones*, V. 1, edited and with introductions by Rabbi Debra Orenstein. Woodstock, VT: Jewish Lights Publishing, 1994. Reprinted by permission of the publisher.

"To the baby I never had," by Reba Carmel. Reprinted by permission of the author.

"Eternal God," by Rabbi Diane Cohen. Reprinted by permission of the author.

"Finding Comfort after a Miscarriage," by Rabbi Susan Grossman, appeared in *Daughters of the King: Women and the Synagogue*, edited by Susan Grossman and Rivka Haut. Philadelphia: Jewish Publication Society, 1992. Reprinted by permission of the publisher.

"Loneliness," by Hannah Senesh, translated by Ruth Finer Mintz, and "Man and Wife," by Shin Shalom, translated by Abraham Birman, appeared in *Love Poems From the Hebrew*, edited by David C. Gross. New York: Doubleday, Garden City, 1976. Reprinted by permission of the editor.

NOTES

Introduction

P. 16   *A woman who lost her child . . . On the Doorposts of Your House: Prayers and Ceremonies for the Jewish Home,* (New York: Central Conference of American Rabbis), 1994, p. 162.

P. 17   *Immediately after that, Sarah, too, conceived.* See Genesis 20–21 and Bava Kama 92a.

P. 21   *I believe better and more thoroughly when I'm singing.* Kathleen Norris, *The Cloister Walk* (New York: Riverhead Books, 1996), p. 330.

Chapter 1—In the Beginning

P. 27   *. . . the pomegranate . . .* I thank Michele Klein for so generously and copiously responding to my query about the pomegranate as a Jewish fertility symbol.

P. 27   *Her "groove. . ."* Marvin H. Pope, *The Anchor Bible, Song of Songs* (New York: Doubleday, 1977), p. 453, line 13a.

P. 30   *You spread Your light over me like a robe. . .* translated and adapted by Nina Beth Cardin, based on Psalm 104.

P. 34   *To my lover* Adapted from "The Song of Glory, *An'im Zemirot,*" from the morning prayers.

Chapter 2—Give Me a Child: Prayers for Conception

P. 40   *Round* Rachel Boimwall, translated by Gabriel Preil and Howard Schwartz, in *Voices Within the Ark: The Modern Jewish Poets,* edited by Howard Schwartz and Anthony Rudolf (New York: Avon Books, 1980).

P. 40   *The Key* Tikva Frymer-Kensky, *Motherprayer: The Pregnant Woman's Spiritual Companion* (New York: Riverhead Books, 1995) pp. 21–22.

P. 43   *Prayer to Rahmana* Penina Adelman, *The Reconstructionist* (April 1985).

P. 45   *If I had a son* Rahel Bluwstein, in *The Plough Woman: Memoirs of the Pioneer Women of Palestine*, edited by Rachel Katznelson-Shazar, translated by Maurice Samuel (New York: Herzl Press, 1975).

P. 46   *God of all creation* . . . Pesikta Rabbati 43:5.

P. 47   *Dear God* . . . Berakhot 31b.

P. 48   *Paired lights proclaim the miracle* . . . Debbie Perlman, "Psalm Sixty-Two," in *Flames to Heaven: New Psalms for Healing and Praise* (Wilmette, IL: RAD Publishers, 1998).

P. 51   *Av Harachaman* . . . Adapted from Eliezer Papo, *Sefer Beit Tefillah* (Jerusalem: Keren Pele Yoetz, 1995), p. 135.

P. 53   *In the name of the Holy One* Adapted from *Lashon Hakhamim L'Maran HaRi"b*, as quoted in Yaakov Moshe Hillel, *Sefer Roni Akarah* (Jerusalem: Ahavat Shalom, 1990).

P. 53   *"Rabbi Yitzchak said . . ."* Rosh Hashanah 16b.

P. 54   *Someone once visited the Chafetz Chayyim* . . . Yisrael Meir ben Aryeh, *Sefer Shem Olam* (Jerusalem: Hamesorah, n.d.), pt. I, chapt 8.

P. 54   *The couple desiring a child* . . . Haben Ish Hai, *Ateret Tiferet*, "Keter Malkhut," section 160, as quoted in *Sefer Roni Akarah*, p. 48.

P. 54   *What can a man do* . . . Bava Batra 10b.

P. 56   *"Changing one's name . . ."* Sefer Roni Akarah, p. 39.

Chapter 3—Prayers for the Holidays

P. 62   *New Year's compote* Adapted from the Epicurious Recipe File, epicurious.com.

P. 63   *Day 1* Pesikta Rabbati 42:7.

P. 63   *Day 2* Ateret Tiferet, as quoted in *Sefer Roni Akarah*, p. 217.

P. 65   *Hospitality*, Tanchuma Ki Tetze 2.

P. 65   *The Shunamite woman*, 2 Kings 4.

P. 65   *and Sarah conceived* . . . Genesis 18.

P. 67   *Geshem* Created by Mark Frydenberg, translated by Rabbi Simchah Roth, unpublished.

P. 68   *Even more, a woman having difficulty giving birth* . . . Rochelle Knebel, of New Milford, NJ, reported this tradition to me during the holiday of Sukkot 5759 in the name of her grandmother.

P. 71   *ken yirbu Ta'amei Himinhagim*, p. 331, as cited in *Sefer Roni Akarah*, p. 55.

Chapter 4—Mourning Loss

P. 77   *Tapping a Stone* Jane Schapiro, *Lilith* (fall, 1989).

P. 78   *The Bath* Lynn E. Levin, *The Reconstructionist* (spring 1993): p. 27.

P. 79   *Healing after a miscarriage* Merle Feld, *A Spiritual Life: A Jewish Feminist Journey* (Albany: SUNY Press, 1997).

P. 82   *We turn the earth* . . . Debbie Perlman, "Eighty-Eight, Rosh Hodesh Sivan," in *Flames to Heaven.*

P. 86   *Hold Me Now* Vicki Hollander, in *Lifecycles: Jewish Women on Life Passages and Personal Milestones*, V. 1, edited and with introductions by Rabbi Debra Orenstein (Woodstock, VT: Jewish Lights Publishing, 1994), p. 46

P. 89   *Turn me toward the light* . . . Debbie Perlman, "Twenty-four," in *Flames to Heaven.*

P. 90   *To the baby I never had* . . . Reba Carmel, unpublished.

P. 92   *Loss* Tikva Frymer-Kensky, *Motherprayer*, pp. 68–69.

P. 94   Rabbi Susan Grossman, "Finding Comfort after a Miscarriage," in *Daughters of the King: Women and the Synagogue*, edited by Susan Grossman and Rivka Haut (Philadelphia: Jewish Publication Society, 1992), pp. 284–290.

P. 95   *May God who blessed our ancestors* . . . Rabbi Amy Eilberg, *Lifecycles*, V. 1, p. 51.

P. 100 *Renew Me Like the Moon* . . . Lois Dubin. A fuller explanation of the structure, texts, and significance of the ceremony can be found in Lois Dubin, "A Ceremony of Remembering, Mourning, and Healing After Miscarriage," *Kerem: Creative Explorations in Judaism*, no. 4 (5756, winter 1995–96): 67–77.

P. 103 *Words of Mourning* Based on the poem by Yehudah Amichai, "*Shenenu be-yahad ve-khol ehad lehud*" ("The Two of Us Together, Each of Us Alone"). In *The Modern Hebrew Poem Itself*, ed. Stanley

Burnshaw, T. Carmi, and Ezra Spicehandler (New York: Schocken Books, 1966).

P. 107 *Eternal God* . . . Rabbi Diane Cohen, unpublished.

P. 109 *O Eternal, hold me with gentleness* . . . Debbie Perlman, "Five" (z"l: E.F.L.), in *Flames to Heaven.*

P. 110 *Ritual for grief* . . . Based on the work of Rabbi Amy Eilberg, "A Grieving Ritual Following Miscarriage or Stillbirth," *Lifecycles,* V. 1, pp. 48–51.

Chapter 5—Helping God Help Us:
Prayers for Medical Intervention

P. 117 *Merciful God* . . . Rabbi Michelle Goldsmith, unpublished.

P. 118 *"As at the Creation of Eve"* Tikva Frymer-Kensky, *Motherprayer,* p. 19.

P. 119 *Out of the depths* . . . Biblical verses selected and translated by Rabbi Diane Cohen

P. 121 *A red stone* Based on the important and pioneering work of Michele Klein, *A Time to Be Born: Jewish Birth Customs and Traditions* (Philadelphia: Jewish Publication Society, 1998). Accompanying prayer, "Dear God, *El Shaddai,*" composed by Nina Beth Cardin.

Chapter 6—Remembering Our Love:
Prayers for Husband and Wife

P. 125 *Loneliness* Hannah Senesh, translated by Ruth Finer Mintz, in *Love Poems from the Hebrew,* edited by David Gross (New York: Doubleday, Garden City, 1976), p. 29.

P. 126 *Seeking you* Chaim Nachman Bialik, translated by Nina Beth Cardin, in *Ahavat Hein, Love Poems: The Love Poetry of Chaim Nachman Bialik* (Hebrew) (Tel Aviv: Modan, 1984).

P. 126 *Man and wife* Shin Shalom, translated by Abraham Birman, in *Love Poems from the Hebrew,* p. 1.

P. 127 *God of all, beloved of the people Israel* . . . Adapted by Nina Beth Cardin from an eighteenth-century Italian women's prayer.

Chapter 7—Pregnancy

P. 130 *Rachel* Barbara Holender, *Sarah's Daughters Sing* (New York: Jewish Women's Resource Center, National Council of Jewish Women, New York Section, 1990).

P. 134 *A prayer for a woman to say so that she not miscarry* Adapted from Yehudah Moshe Patya, *Hasdei David*, as quoted in *Sefer Roni Akarah*, p. 137.

P. 135 *I beseech You . . .* Adapted from *The Merit of our Mothers: A Bilingual Anthology of Jewish Women's Prayers*, compiled and introduced by Tracy Guren Klirs (Cincinnati: Hebrew Union College Press, 1992), p. 124.

P. 135 *Master of the World . . .* Adapted from Eliezer Papo, *Sefer Beit Tefillah*, pp. 134–138.

P. 136 *M'ugelet* Rabbi Jane R. Litman, in *A Ceremonies Sampler: New Rites, Celebrations, and Observances of Jewish Women*, edited by Elizabeth Resnick Levine (San Diego: Women's Institute for Continuing Jewish Education, 1991). For more information on the cult of Rachel Our Mother, see Susan Sered, "A Tale of Three Rachels," *Nashim: A Journal of Jewish Women's Studies and Gender Issues, no. 1* (winter 5758/1998.)

P. 138 *Lord our God . . .* Based on a prayer found in book 4433b in the Rare Book Collection of the Jewish Theological Seminary Rare Book Room.

P. 138 *To prepare themselves. . .* Nina Beth Cardin, *Out of the Depths I Call to You: A Book of Prayers for the Married Jewish Woman*, (Northvale, NJ: Jason Aronson, 1995), pp. 84–85.

P. 139 *I thank You God . . .* Based on prayers from the Italian Jewish tradition.

P. 141 *It is I . . .* Adapted from Isa. 51:12–52:12.

P. 141 *Gracious, awesome, and mighty God . . .* Based on p. 97 ff. from *Ma'aneh Lashon*, 1913.

P. 143 *May it be Your will . . .* A blend of prayers from *Siddur HaAri, Shaarei Rahamim—Hameuyhas Lra"h Hakohen* p. 102b, and *Out of the Depths I Call to You: A Book of Prayers for the Married Jewish Woman*, p. 61.

Chapter 8—Stillbirth and Death

P. 149 *Funeral for a stillborn* . . . Adapted from the work of Rabbi Amy Eilberg, *Lifecycles*, V. 1, pp. 48–51.

P. 151 *Dear God, Healer of the broken-hearted* . . . Based on a prayer by Rabbi Perry Raphael Rank.

P. 152 *Yizkor* Rabbi Ira Stone, *Kerem* (winter 1994), pp. 86–87.

P. 152 *A Father's Lament* David Morawetz, *Go Gently: A Parent's Grief* (Omaha, NB: Centering Corporation, 1991).

P. 154 *Lament of a grandparent* Mel Isaacs, in *Confronting the Loss of a Baby: A Jewish and Personal Perspective*, by Yamin Levy (Hoboken, NJ: KTAV, 1998).

P. 155 *Some people give me advice* David Morawetz, *Go Gently*.

Chapter 9—Finding Peace

P. 158 *"When a barren man . . ."* *Tachuma, Parashat Noach*.

P. 159 *A couple in which the wife is infertile* . . . Yaakov Moshe Hillel, *Sefer Roni Akarah*, p. 75.

P. 160 *Precious Gift* Shir Hashirim Rabba 1:31.

P. 161 *Kaddish* Rabbi Geela Rayzel Raphael, unpublished.

P. 164 *"Draw me close . . ."* Chayyim Nachman, from the poem *"Hakhnisini tachat Kenafekh."*

P. 165 *A Tashlikh ritual for accepting infertility* Inspired by Bonnie and Lawrence Baron, *"Seder Kabbalat Ahkaroot,"* in *A Ceremonies Sampler: New Rites, Celebrations, and Observances of Jewish Women*.

P. 168 *We have been blessed* . . . Rabbi Sandy Sasso, *Lifecycles*, V. 1, p. 33.

Epilogue—Eve and Deborah: Of Mothers, Mamas, Mothering

P. 171 *The aunties, the sisters* Lorraine Johnson-Coleman, *Just Plain Folks* (Boston: Little, Brown & Co., 1998), pp. 59–60.

Journaling

Journaling

Journaling

Journaling

Journaling

Journaling

Journaling

Bar/Bat Mitzvah

The JGirl's Guide: The Young Jewish Woman's Handbook for Coming of Age
By Penina Adelman, Ali Feldman, and Shulamit Reinharz
An inspirational, interactive guidebook designed to help pre-teen Jewish girls address the spiritual, educational, and psychological issues surrounding coming of age in today's society.   6 x 9, 240 pp, Quality PB, 978-1-58023-215-9 **$14.99**
  Also Available: **The JGirl's Teacher's and Parent's Guide**
  8½ x 11, 56 pp, PB, 978-1-58023-225-8 **$8.99**

Bar/Bat Mitzvah Basics: A Practical Family Guide to Coming of Age Together
Edited by Cantor Helen Leneman 6 x 9, 240 pp, Quality PB, 978-1-58023-151-0 **$18.95**

The Bar/Bat Mitzvah Memory Book, 2nd Edition: An Album for Treasuring the Spiritual Celebration *By Rabbi Jeffrey K. Salkin and Nina Salkin*
8 x 10, 48 pp, Deluxe HC, 2-color text, ribbon marker, 978-1-58023-263-0 **$19.99**

For Kids—Putting God on Your Guest List: How to Claim the Spiritual Meaning of Your Bar or Bat Mitzvah *By Rabbi Jeffrey K. Salkin*
6 x 9, 144 pp, Quality PB, 978-1-58023-015-5 **$14.99** *For ages 11–13*

Putting God on the Guest List, 3rd Edition: How to Reclaim the Spiritual Meaning of Your Child's Bar or Bat Mitzvah *By Rabbi Jeffrey K. Salkin*
6 x 9, 224 pp, Quality PB, 978-1-58023-222-7 **$16.99**; HC, 978-1-58023-260-9 **$24.99**
Also Available: **Putting God on the Guest List Teacher's Guide**
8½ x 11, 48 pp, PB, 978-1-58023-226-5 **$8.99**

Tough Questions Jews Ask: A Young Adult's Guide to Building a Jewish Life
By Rabbi Edward Feinstein 6 x 9, 160 pp, Quality PB, 978-1-58023-139-8 **$14.99** *For ages 12 & up*
Also Available: **Tough Questions Jews Ask Teacher's Guide**
8½ x 11, 72 pp, PB, 978-1-58023-187-9 **$8.95**

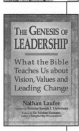

Bible Study/Midrash

Abraham's Bind & Other Bible Tales of Trickery, Folly, Mercy and Love *By Michael J. Caduto*
Re-imagines many biblical characters, retelling their stories and highlighting their foibles and strengths, their struggles and joys. Readers will learn that God has a way of working for them and through them, even today.
6 x 9, 224 pp, HC, 978-1-59473-186-0 **$19.99** *(A SkyLight Paths book)*

Ancient Secrets: Using the Stories of the Bible to Improve Our Everyday Lives
By Rabbi Levi Meier, PhD 5½ x 8½, 288 pp, Quality PB, 978-1-58023-064-3 **$16.95**

The Genesis of Leadership: What the Bible Teaches Us about Vision, Values and Leading Change *By Rabbi Nathan Laufer; Foreword by Senator Joseph I. Lieberman*
Unlike other books on leadership, this one is rooted in the stories of the Bible, and teaches the values that the Bible believes are prerequisites for true leadership.
6 x 9, 288 pp, HC, 978-1-58023-241-8 **$24.99**

Hineini in Our Lives: Learning How to Respond to Others through 14 Biblical Texts and Personal Stories *By Norman J. Cohen* 6 x 9, 240 pp, Quality PB, 978-1-58023-274-6 **$16.99**

Moses and the Journey to Leadership: Timeless Lessons of Effective Management from the Bible and Today's Leaders *By Dr. Norman J. Cohen* 6 x 9, 250 pp, HC, 978-1-58023-227-2 **$21.99**

Self, Struggle & Change: Family Conflict Stories in Genesis and Their Healing Insights for Our Lives *By Norman J. Cohen* 6 x 9, 224 pp, Quality PB, 978-1-879045-66-8 **$18.99**

The Triumph of Eve & Other Subversive Bible Tales *By Matt Biers-Ariel*
5½ x 8½, 192 pp, HC, 978-1-59473-040-5 **$19.99** *(A SkyLight Paths book)*

Voices from Genesis: Guiding Us through the Stages of Life *By Norman J. Cohen*
6 x 9, 192 pp, Quality PB, 978-1-58023-118-3 **$16.95**

Congregation Resources

The Art of Public Prayer, 2nd Edition: Not for Clergy Only *By Lawrence A. Hoffman*
6 x 9, 272 pp, Quality PB, 978-1-893361-06-5 **$19.99** *(A SkyLight Paths book)*

Becoming a Congregation of Learners: Learning as a Key to Revitalizing
Congregational Life *By Isa Aron, PhD; Foreword by Rabbi Lawrence A. Hoffman*
6 x 9, 304 pp, Quality PB, 978-1-58023-089-6 **$19.95**

Finding a Spiritual Home: How a New Generation of Jews Can Transform the
American Synagogue *By Rabbi Sidney Schwarz*
6 x 9, 352 pp, Quality PB, 978-1-58023-185-5 **$19.95**

Jewish Pastoral Care, 2nd Edition: A Practical Handbook from Traditional &
Contemporary Sources *Edited by Rabbi Dayle A. Friedman*
6 x 9, 528 pp, HC, 978-1-58023-221-0 **$40.00**

Jewish Spiritual Direction: An Innovative Guide from Traditional and Contemporary
Sources *Edited by Rabbi Howard A. Addison and Barbara Eve Breitman*
6 x 9, 368 pp, HC, 978-1-58023-230-2 **$30.00**

The Self-Renewing Congregation: Organizational Strategies for Revitalizing
Congregational Life *By Isa Aron, PhD; Foreword by Dr. Ron Wolfson*
6 x 9, 304 pp, Quality PB, 978-1-58023-166-4 **$19.95**

Spiritual Community: The Power to Restore Hope, Commitment and Joy
By Rabbi David A. Teutsch, PhD 5½ x 8½, 144 pp, HC, 978-1-58023-270-8 **$19.99**

The Spirituality of Welcoming: How to Transform Your Congregation into a
Sacred Community *By Dr. Ron Wolfson* 6 x 9, 224 pp, Quality PB, 978-1-58023-244-9 **$19.99**

Rethinking Synagogues: A New Vocabulary for Congregational Life
By Rabbi Lawrence A. Hoffman 6 x 9, 240 pp, Quality PB, 978-1-58023-248-7 **$19.99**

Children's Books

What You Will See Inside a Synagogue
By Rabbi Lawrence A. Hoffman and Dr. Ron Wolfson; Full-color photos by Bill Aron
A colorful, fun-to-read introduction that explains the ways and whys of Jewish
worship and religious life.
8½ x 10½, 32 pp, Full-color photos, HC, 978-1-59473-012-2 **$17.99** *For ages 6 & up (A SkyLight Paths book)*

The Kids' Fun Book of Jewish Time
By Emily Sper 9 x 7½, 24 pp, Full-color illus., HC, 978-1-58023-311-8 **$16.99**

In God's Hands
By Lawrence Kushner and Gary Schmidt 9 x 12, 32 pp, HC, 978-1-58023-224-1 **$16.99**

Because Nothing Looks Like God
By Lawrence and Karen Kushner
Introduces children to the possibilities of spiritual life.
11 x 8½, 32 pp, Full-color illus., HC, 978-1-58023-092-6 **$16.95** *For ages 4 & up*

Also Available: **Because Nothing Looks Like God Teacher's Guide**
8½ x 11, 22 pp, PB, 978-1-58023-140-4 **$6.95** *For ages 5–8*
 Board Book Companions to *Because Nothing Looks Like God*
5 x 5, 24 pp, Full-color illus., SkyLight Paths Board Books *For ages 0–4*

What Does God Look Like? 978-1-893361-23-2 **$7.99**
How Does God Make Things Happen? 978-1-893361-24-9 **$7.95**
Where Is God? 978-1-893361-17-1 **$7.99**

The Book of Miracles: A Young Person's Guide to Jewish Spiritual Awareness
By Lawrence Kushner. All-new illustrations by the author
6 x 9, 96 pp, 2-color illus., HC, 978-1-879045-78-1 **$16.95** *For ages 9 and up*

In Our Image: God's First Creatures
By Nancy Sohn Swartz 9 x 12, 32 pp, Full-color illus., HC, 978-1-879045-99-6 **$16.95** *For ages 4 & up*

Also Available as a Board Book: **How Did the Animals Help God?**
5 x 5, 24 pp, Board, Full-color illus., 978-1-59473-044-3 **$7.99** *For ages 0–4 (A SkyLight Paths book)*

Children's Books
by Sandy Eisenberg Sasso

Adam & Eve's First Sunset: God's New Day
Engaging new story explores fear and hope, faith and gratitude in ways that will delight kids and adults—inspiring us to bless each of God's days and nights.
9 x 12, 32 pp, Full-color illus., HC, 978-1-58023-177-0 **$17.95** *For ages 4 & up*

Also Available as a Board Book: **Adam and Eve's New Day**
5 x 5, 24 pp, Full-color illus., Board, 978-1-59473-205-8 **$7.99** *For ages 0–4 (A SkyLight Paths book)*

But God Remembered
Stories of Women from Creation to the Promised Land
Four different stories of women—Lillith, Serach, Bityah, and the Daughters of Z—teach us important values through their faith and actions.
9 x 12, 32 pp, Full-color illus., HC, 978-1-879045-43-9 **$16.95** *For ages 8 & up*

Cain & Abel: Finding the Fruits of Peace
Shows children that we have the power to deal with anger in positive ways. Provides questions for kids and adults to explore together.
9 x 12, 32 pp, Full-color illus., HC, 978-1-58023-123-7 **$16.95** *For ages 5 & up*

God in Between
If you wanted to find God, where would you look? This magical, mythical tale teaches that God can be found where we are: within all of us and the relationships between us.
9 x 12, 32 pp, Full-color illus., HC, 978-1-879045-86-6 **$16.95** *For ages 4 & up*

God's Paintbrush: Special 10th Anniversary Edition
Wonderfully interactive, invites children of all faiths and backgrounds to encounter God through moments in their own lives. Provides questions adult and child can explore together.
11 x 8½, 32 pp, Full-color illus., HC, 978-1-58023-195-4 **$17.95** *For ages 4 & up*

Also Available: **God's Paintbrush Teacher's Guide**
8½ x 11, 32 pp, PB, 978-1-879045-57-6 **$8.95**

God's Paintbrush Celebration Kit
A Spiritual Activity Kit for Teachers and Students of All Faiths, All Backgrounds
Additional activity sheets available:
8-Student Activity Sheet Pack (40 sheets/5 sessions), 978-1-58023-058-2 **$19.95**
Single-Student Activity Sheet Pack (5 sessions), 978-1-58023-059-9 **$3.95**

In God's Name
Like an ancient myth in its poetic text and vibrant illustrations, this award-winning modern fable about the search for God's name celebrates the diversity and, at the same time, the unity of all people.
9 x 12, 32 pp, Full-color illus., HC, 978-1-879045-26-2 **$16.99** *For ages 4 & up*

Also Available as a Board Book: **What Is God's Name?**
5 x 5, 24 pp, Board, Full-color illus., 978-1-893361-10-2 **$7.99** *For ages 0–4 (A SkyLight Paths book)*

Also Available: **In God's Name video and study guide**
Computer animation, original music, and children's voices. 18 min. **$29.99**

Also Available in Spanish: **El nombre de Dios**
9 x 12, 32 pp, Full-color illus., HC, 978-1-893361-63-8 **$16.95** *(A SkyLight Paths book)*

Noah's Wife: The Story of Naamah
When God tells Noah to bring the animals of the world onto the ark, God also calls on Naamah, Noah's wife, to save each plant on Earth. Based on an ancient text.
9 x 12, 32 pp, Full-color illus., HC, 978-1-58023-134-3 **$16.95** *For ages 4 & up*

Also Available as a Board Book: **Naamah, Noah's Wife**
5 x 5, 24 pp, Full-color illus., Board, 978-1-893361-56-0 **$7.95** *For ages 0–4 (A SkyLight Paths book)*

For Heaven's Sake: Finding God in Unexpected Places
9 x 12, 32 pp, Full-color illus., HC, 978-1-58023-054-4 **$16.95** *For ages 4 & up*

God Said Amen: Finding the Answers to Our Prayers
9 x 12, 32 pp, Full-color illus., HC, 978-1-58023-080-3 **$16.95** *For ages 4 & up*

Theology/Philosophy

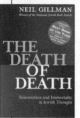

Christians and Jews in Dialogue: Learning in the Presence of the Other
By Mary C. Boys and Sara S. Lee; Foreword by Dr. Dorothy Bass
6 x 9, 240 pp, HC, 978-1-59473-144-0 **$21.99** (A SkyLight Paths book)

The Death of Death: Resurrection and Immortality in Jewish Thought
By Neil Gillman   6 x 9, 336 pp, Quality PB, 978-1-58023-081-0 **$18.95**

Ethics of the Sages: Pirke Avot—Annotated & Explained
Translation & Annotation by Rabbi Rami Shapiro
5½ x 8½, 208 pp, Quality PB, 978-1-59473-207-2 **$16.99** (A SkyLight Paths book)

Evolving Halakhah: A Progressive Approach to Traditional Jewish Law
By Rabbi Dr. Moshe Zemer 6 x 9, 480 pp, Quality PB, 978-1-58023-127-5 **$29.95**;
HC, 978-1-58023-002-5 **$40.00**

Hasidic Tales: Annotated & Explained
By Rabbi Rami Shapiro; Foreword by Andrew Harvey
5½ x 8½, 240 pp, Quality PB, 978-1-893361-86-7 **$16.95** (A SkyLight Paths Book)

Healing the Jewish-Christian Rift: Growing Beyond our Wounded History
By Ron Miller and Laura Bernstein; Foreword by Dr. Beatrice Bruteau
6 x 9, 288 pp, Quality PB, 978-1-59473-139-6 **$18.99** (A SkyLight Paths book)

A Heart of Many Rooms: Celebrating the Many Voices within Judaism
By David Hartman 6 x 9, 352 pp, Quality PB, 978-1-58023-156-5 **$19.95**

The Hebrew Prophets: Selections Annotated & Explained
Translation & Annotation by Rabbi Rami Shapiro; Foreword by Zalman M. Schachter-Shalomi
5½ x 8½, 224 pp, Quality PB, 978-1-59473-037-5 **$16.99** (A SkyLight Paths book)

A Jewish Understanding of the New Testament
By Rabbi Samuel Sandmel; Preface by Rabbi David Sandmel
5½ x 8½, 368 pp, Quality PB, 978-1-59473-048-1 **$19.99** (A SkyLight Paths book)

Keeping Faith with the Psalms: Deepen Your Relationship with God Using the Book
of Psalms By Daniel F. Polish 6 x 9, 320 pp, Quality PB, 978-1-58023-300-2 **$18.99**;
HC, 978-1-58023-179-4 **$24.95**

A Living Covenant: The Innovative Spirit in Traditional Judaism
By David Hartman 6 x 9, 368 pp, Quality PB, 978-1-58023-011-7 **$20.00**

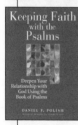

Love and Terror in the God Encounter
The Theological Legacy of Rabbi Joseph B. Soloveitchik
By David Hartman 6 x 9, 240 pp, Quality PB, 978-1-58023-176-3 **$19.95**;
HC, 978-1-58023-112-1 **$25.00**

The Personhood of God: Biblical Theology, Human Faith and the Divine Image
By Dr. Yochanan Muffs; Foreword by Dr. David Hartman
6 x 9, 240 pp, HC, 978-1-58023-265-4 **$24.99**

Tormented Master: The Life and Spiritual Quest of Rabbi Nahman of Bratslav
By Arthur Green 6 x 9, 416 pp, Quality PB, 978-1-879045-11-8 **$19.99**

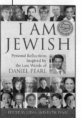

Traces of God: Seeing God in Torah, History and Everyday Life
By Neil Gillman 6 x 9, 240 pp, HC, 978-1-58023-249-4 **$21.99**

We Jews and Jesus: Exploring Theological Differences for Mutual Understanding
By Rabbi Samuel Sandmel; Preface by Rabbi David Sandmel
6 x 9, 176 pp, Quality PB, 978-1-59473-208-9 **$16.99** (A SkyLight Paths book)

Your Word Is Fire: The Hasidic Masters on Contemplative Prayer
Edited and translated by Arthur Green and Barry W. Holtz
6 x 9, 160 pp, Quality PB, 978-1-879045-25-5 **$15.95**

I Am Jewish
Personal Reflections Inspired by the Last Words of Daniel Pearl
Almost 150 Jews—both famous and not—from all walks of life, from all around
the world, write about Identity, Heritage, Covenant / Chosenness and Faith,
Humanity and Ethnicity, and *Tikkun Olam* and Justice.
Edited by Judea and Ruth Pearl
6 x 9, 304 pp, Deluxe PB w/flaps, 978-1-58023-259-3 **$18.99**; HC, 978-1-58023-183-1 **$24.99**
Download a free copy of the *I Am Jewish Teacher's Guide* at our website:
www.jewishlights.com

Theology/Philosophy/The Way Into... Series

The Way Into... series offers an accessible and highly usable "guided tour" of the Jewish faith, people, history and beliefs—in total, an introduction to Judaism that will enable you to understand and interact with the sacred texts of the Jewish tradition. Each volume is written by a leading contemporary scholar and teacher, and explores one key aspect of Judaism. *The Way Into...* series enables all readers to achieve a real sense of Jewish cultural literacy through guided study.

The Way Into Encountering God in Judaism
By Neil Gillman
For everyone who wants to understand how Jews have encountered God throughout history and today.
6 x 9, 240 pp, Quality PB, 978-1-58023-199-2 **$18.99**; HC, 978-1-58023-025-4 **$21.95**
Also Available: **The Jewish Approach to God:** A Brief Introduction for Christians
By Neil Gillman
5½ x 8½, 192 pp, Quality PB, 978-1-58023-190-9 **$16.95**

The Way Into Jewish Mystical Tradition
By Lawrence Kushner
Allows readers to interact directly with the sacred mystical text of the Jewish tradition. An accessible introduction to the concepts of Jewish mysticism, their religious and spiritual significance and how they relate to life today.
6 x 9, 224 pp, Quality PB, 978-1-58023-200-5 **$18.99**; HC, 978-1-58023-029-2 **$21.95**

The Way Into Jewish Prayer
By Lawrence A. Hoffman
Opens the door to 3,000 years of Jewish prayer, making available all anyone needs to feel at home in the Jewish way of communicating with God.
6 x 9, 224 pp, Quality PB, 978-1-58023-201-2 **$18.99**

The Way Into Judaism and the Environment
By Jeremy Benstein
Explores the ways in which Judaism contributes to contemporary social-environmental issues, the extent to which Judaism is part of the problem and how it can be part of the solution.
6 x 9, 288 pp, HC, 978-1-58023-268-5 **$24.99**

The Way Into *Tikkun Olam* (Repairing the World)
By Elliot N. Dorff
An accessible introduction to the Jewish concept of the individual's responsibility to care for others and repair the world.
6 x 9, 320 pp, HC, 978-1-58023-269-2 **$24.99**

The Way Into Torah
By Norman J. Cohen
Helps guide in the exploration of the origins and development of Torah, explains why it should be studied and how to do it.
6 x 9, 176 pp, Quality PB, 978-1-58023-198-5 **$16.99**; HC, 978-1-58023-028-5 **$21.95**

The Way Into the Varieties of Jewishness
By Sylvia Barack Fishman, PhD
Explores the religious and historical understanding of what it has meant to be Jewish from ancient times to the present controversy over "Who is a Jew?"
6 x 9, 288 pp, HC, 978-1-58023-030-8 **$24.99**

Current Events/History

The Story of the Jews: A 4,000-Year Adventure—A Graphic History Book
Written & illustrated by Stan Mack
Witty, illustrated narrative of all the major happenings from biblical times to the
twenty-first century. 6 x 9, 288 pp, illus., Quality PB, 978-1-58023-155-8 **$16.95**

Hannah Senesh: Her Life and Diary, the First Complete Edition
By Hannah Senesh; Foreword by Marge Piercy; Preface by Eitan Senesh
6 x 9, 352 pp, HC, 978-1-58023-212-8 **$24.99**

The Jewish Prophet: Visionary Words from Moses and Miriam to Henrietta Szold
and A. J. Heschel By Rabbi Dr. Michael J. Shire
6½ x 8½, 128 pp, 123 full-color illus., HC, 978-1-58023-168-8
Special gift price **$14.95**

Foundations of Sephardic Spirituality: The Inner Life of Jews of the Ottoman Empire
By Rabbi Marc D. Angel, PhD 6 x 9, 224 pp, HC, 978-1-58023-243-2 **$24.99**

Judaism and Justice: The Jewish Passion to Repair the World
By Rabbi Sidney Schwarz
6 x 9, 250 pp, HC, 978-1-58023-312-5 **$24.99**

Ecology

Ecology & the Jewish Spirit: Where Nature & the Sacred Meet
Edited by Ellen Bernstein 6 x 9, 288 pp, Quality PB, 978-1-58023-082-7 **$16.95**

Torah of the Earth: Exploring 4,000 Years of Ecology in Jewish Thought
Vol. 1: Biblical Israel: One Land, One People; Rabbinic Judaism: One People, Many Lands
Vol. 2: Zionism: One Land, Two Peoples; Eco-Judaism: One Earth, Many Peoples
Edited by Arthur Waskow
Vol. 1: 6 x 9, 272 pp, Quality PB, 978-1-58023-086-5 **$19.95**
Vol. 2: 6 x 9, 336 pp, Quality PB, 978-1-58023-087-2 **$19.95**

The Way Into Judaism and the Environment
By Jeremy Benstein 6 x 9, 224 pp, HC, 978-1-58023-268-5 **$24.99**

Grief/Healing

Against the Dying of the Light: A Parent's Story of Love, Loss and Hope
By Leonard Fein
5½ x 8½, 176 pp, Quality PB, 978-1-58023-197-8 **$15.99**

Grief in Our Seasons: A Mourner's Kaddish Companion By Rabbi Kerry M. Olitzky
4½ x 6½, 448 pp, Quality PB, 978-1-879045-55-2 **$15.95**

Healing of Soul, Healing of Body: Spiritual Leaders Unfold the Strength & Solace
in Psalms Edited by Rabbi Simkha Y. Weintraub, CSW
6 x 9, 128 pp, 2-color illus. text, Quality PB, 978-1-879045-31-6 **$14.99**

Jewish Paths toward Healing and Wholeness: A Personal Guide to Dealing with
Suffering By Rabbi Kerry M. Olitzky; Foreword by Debbie Friedman.
6 x 9, 192 pp, Quality PB, 978-1-58023-068-1 **$15.95**

Mourning & Mitzvah, 2nd Edition: A Guided Journal for Walking the Mourner's
Path through Grief to Healing By Anne Brener, LCSW
7½ x 9, 304 pp, Quality PB, 978-1-58023-113-8 **$19.99**

The Perfect Stranger's Guide to Funerals and Grieving Practices
A Guide to Etiquette in Other People's Religious Ceremonies Edited by Stuart M. Matlins
6 x 9, 240 pp, Quality PB, 978-1-893361-20-1 **$16.95** (A SkyLight Paths book)

Tears of Sorrow, Seeds of Hope, 2nd Edition: A Jewish Spiritual Companion for
Infertility and Pregnancy Loss By Rabbi Nina Beth Cardin
6 x 9, 208 pp, Quality PB, 978-1-58023-233-3 **$18.99**

A Time to Mourn, A Time to Comfort, 2nd Edition: A Guide to Jewish
Bereavement By Dr. Ron Wolfson
7 x 9, 384 pp, Quality PB, 978-1-58023-253-1 **$19.99**

When a Grandparent Dies: A Kid's Own Remembering Workbook for Dealing
with Shiva and the Year Beyond By Nechama Liss-Levinson, PhD
8 x 10, 48 pp, 2-color text, HC, 978-1-879045-44-6 **$15.95** For ages 7–13

Meditation

The Handbook of Jewish Meditation Practices
A Guide for Enriching the Sabbath and Other Days of Your Life
By Rabbi David A. Cooper Easy-to-learn meditation techniques.
6 x 9, 208 pp, Quality PB, 978-1-58023-102-2 **$16.95**

Discovering Jewish Meditation: Instruction & Guidance for Learning an Ancient
Spiritual Practice *By Nan Fink Gefen*
6 x 9, 208 pp, Quality PB, 978-1-58023-067-4 **$16.95**

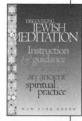

A Heart of Stillness: A Complete Guide to Learning the Art of Meditation
By David A. Cooper 5½ x 8½, 272 pp, Quality PB, 978-1-893361-03-4 **$16.95** *(A SkyLight Paths book)*

Meditation from the Heart of Judaism: Today's Teachers Share Their
Practices, Techniques, and Faith *Edited by Avram Davis*
6 x 9, 256 pp, Quality PB, 978-1-58023-049-0 **$16.95**

Silence, Simplicity & Solitude: A Complete Guide to Spiritual Retreat at Home
By David A. Cooper 5½ x 8½, 336 pp, Quality PB, 978-1-893361-04-1 **$16.95**
(A SkyLight Paths book)

The Way of Flame: A Guide to the Forgotten Mystical Tradition of Jewish
Meditation *By Avram Davis* 4½ x 8, 176 pp, Quality PB, 978-1-58023-060-5 **$15.95**

Ritual/Sacred Practice/Journaling

The Jewish Dream Book: The Key to Opening the Inner Meaning of
Your Dreams *By Vanessa L. Ochs with Elizabeth Ochs; Full-color illus. by Kristina Swarner*
Instructions for how modern people can perform ancient Jewish dream practices
and dream interpretations drawn from the Jewish wisdom tradition.
8 x 8, 128 pp, Full-color illus., Deluxe PB w/flaps, 978-1-58023-132-9 **$16.95**

The Jewish Journaling Book: How to Use Jewish Tradition to Write
Your Life & Explore Your Soul *By Janet Ruth Falon*
Details the history of Jewish journaling throughout biblical and modern times, and
teaches specific journaling techniques to help you create and maintain a vital journal,
from a Jewish perspective. 8 x 8, 304 pp, Deluxe PB w/flaps, 978-1-58023-203-6 **$18.99**

The Book of Jewish Sacred Practices: CLAL's Guide to Everyday & Holiday
Rituals & Blessings *Edited by Rabbi Irwin Kula and Vanessa L. Ochs, PhD*
6 x 9, 368 pp, Quality PB, 978-1-58023-152-7 **$18.95**

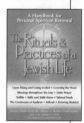

Jewish Ritual: A Brief Introduction for Christians
By Rabbi Kerry M. Olitzky and Rabbi Daniel Judson
5½ x 8½, 144 pp, Quality PB, 978-1-58023-210-4 **$14.99**

The Rituals & Practices of a Jewish Life: A Handbook for Personal Spiritual
Renewal *Edited by Rabbi Kerry M. Olitzky and Rabbi Daniel Judson*
6 x 9, 272 pp, illus., Quality PB, 978-1-58023-169-5 **$18.95**

The Sacred Art of Lovingkindness: Preparing to Practice
By Rabbi Rami Shapiro 5½ x 8½, 176 pp, Quality PB, 978-1-59473-151-8 **$16.99**
(A SkyLight Paths book)

Science Fiction/Mystery & Detective Fiction

Mystery Midrash: An Anthology of Jewish Mystery & Detective Fiction
Edited by Lawrence W. Raphael; Preface by Joel Siegel
6 x 9, 304 pp, Quality PB, 978-1-58023-055-1 **$16.95**

Criminal Kabbalah: An Intriguing Anthology of Jewish Mystery & Detective Fiction
Edited by Lawrence W. Raphael; Foreword by Laurie R. King
6 x 9, 256 pp, Quality PB, 978-1-58023-109-1 **$16.95**

Wandering Stars: An Anthology of Jewish Fantasy & Science Fiction
Edited by Jack Dann; Introduction by Isaac Asimov
6 x 9, 272 pp, Quality PB, 978-1-58023-005-6 **$16.95**

More Wandering Stars: An Anthology of Outstanding Stories of Jewish Fantasy and
Science Fiction *Edited by Jack Dann; Introduction by Isaac Asimov*
6 x 9, 192 pp, Quality PB, 978-1-58023-063-6 **$16.95**

Spirituality

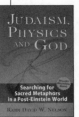

The Adventures of Rabbi Harvey: A Graphic Novel of Jewish Wisdom and Wit in the Wild West *By Steve Sheinkin*
Jewish and American folktales combine in this witty and original graphic novel collection. Creatively retold and set on the western frontier of the 1870s.
6 x 9, 144 pp, Full-color illus., Quality PB, 978-1-58023-310-1 **$16.99**
Also Available: **The Adventures of Rabbi Harvey Teacher's Guide**
8½ x 11, 32 pp, PB, 978-1-58023-326-2 **$8.99**

Ethics of the Sages: *Pirke Avot*—Annotated & Explained
Translation and Annotation by Rabbi Rami Shapiro
5½ x 8¼, 192 pp, Quality PB, 978-1-59473-207-2 **$16.99** (A SkyLight Paths book)

A Book of Life: Embracing Judaism as a Spiritual Practice
By Michael Strassfeld 6 x 9, 528 pp, Quality PB, 978-1-58023-247-0 **$19.99**

Meaning and Mitzvah: Daily Practices for Reclaiming Judaism through Prayer, God, Torah, Hebrew, Mitzvot and Peoplehood *By Rabbi Goldie Milgram*
7 x 9, 336 pp, Quality PB, 978-1-58023-256-2 **$19.99**

The Soul of the Story: Meetings with Remarkable People
By Rabbi David Zeller 6 x 9, 288 pp, HC, 978-1-58023-272-2 **$21.99**

Aleph-Bet Yoga: Embodying the Hebrew Letters for Physical and Spiritual Well-Being
By Steven A. Rapp. Foreword by Tamar Frankiel, PhD and Judy Greenfeld. Preface by Hart Lazer.
7 x 10, 128 pp, b/w photos, Quality PB, Layflat binding, 978-1-58023-162-6 **$16.95**

Entering the Temple of Dreams: Jewish Prayers, Movements, and Meditations for the End of the Day *By Tamar Frankiel, PhD, and Judy Greenfeld*
7 x 10, 192 pp, illus., Quality PB, 978-1-58023-079-7 **$16.95**

Does the Soul Survive? A Jewish Journey to Belief in Afterlife, Past Lives & Living with Purpose *By Rabbi Elie Kaplan Spitz; Foreword by Brian L. Weiss, MD*
6 x 9, 288 pp, Quality PB, 978-1-58023-165-7 **$16.99**

First Steps to a New Jewish Spirit: Reb Zalman's Guide to Recapturing the Intimacy & Ecstasy in Your Relationship with God *By Rabbi Zalman M. Schachter-Shalomi with Donald Gropman* 6 x 9, 144 pp, Quality PB, 978-1-58023-182-4 **$16.95**

God in Our Relationships: Spirituality between People from the Teachings of Martin Buber *By Rabbi Dennis S. Ross* 5½ x 8¼, 160 pp, Quality PB, 978-1-58023-147-3 **$16.95**

Judaism, Physics and God: Searching for Sacred Metaphors in a Post-Einstein World
By Rabbi David W. Nelson 6 x 9, 368 pp, Quality PB, inc. reader's discussion guide, 978-1-58023-306-4 **$18.99**;
HC, 352 pp, 978-1-58023-252-4 **$24.99**

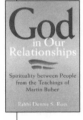

The Jewish Lights Spirituality Handbook: A Guide to Understanding, Exploring & Living a Spiritual Life *Edited by Stuart M. Matlins*
What exactly is "Jewish" about spirituality? How do I make it a part of my life? Fifty of today's foremost spiritual leaders share their ideas and experience with us.
6 x 9, 456 pp, Quality PB, 978-1-58023-093-3 **$19.99**

Bringing the Psalms to Life: How to Understand and Use the Book of Psalms
By Daniel F. Polish 6 x 9, 208 pp, Quality PB, 978-1-58023-157-2 **$16.95**;
HC, 978-1-58023-077-3 **$21.95**

God & the Big Bang: Discovering Harmony between Science & Spirituality
By Daniel C. Matt 6 x 9, 216 pp, Quality PB, 978-1-879045-89-7 **$16.99**

Minding the Temple of the Soul: Balancing Body, Mind, and Spirit through Traditional Jewish Prayer, Movement, and Meditation *By Tamar Frankiel, PhD, and Judy Greenfeld*
7 x 10, 184 pp, illus., Quality PB, 978-1-879045-64-4 **$16.95**
Audiotape of the Blessings and Meditations: 60 min. **$9.95**
Videotape of the Movements and Meditations: 46 min. **$20.00**

One God Clapping: The Spiritual Path of a Zen Rabbi *By Alan Lew with Sherril Jaffe*
5½ x 8¼, 336 pp, Quality PB, 978-1-58023-115-2 **$16.95**

There Is No Messiah ... and You're It: The Stunning Transformation of Judaism's Most Provocative Idea *By Rabbi Robert N. Levine, DD*
6 x 9, 192 pp, Quality PB, 978-1-58023-255-5 **$16.99**

These Are the Words: A Vocabulary of Jewish Spiritual Life
By Arthur Green 6 x 9, 304 pp, Quality PB, 978-1-58023-107-7 **$18.95**

Spirituality/Lawrence Kushner

Filling Words with Light: Hasidic and Mystical Reflections on Jewish Prayer
By Lawrence Kushner and Nehemia Polen
5½ x 8½, 176 pp, HC, 978-1-58023-216-6 **$21.99**

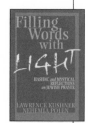

The Book of Letters: A Mystical Hebrew Alphabet
Popular HC Edition, 6 x 9, 80 pp, 2-color text, 978-1-879045-00-2 **$24.95**
Collector's Limited Edition, 9 x 12, 80 pp, gold foil embossed pages, w/limited edition silkscreened
print, 978-1-879045-04-0 **$349.00**

The Book of Miracles: A Young Person's Guide to Jewish Spiritual Awareness
6 x 9, 96 pp, 2-color illus., HC, 978-1-879045-78-1 **$16.95** *For ages 9 and up*

The Book of Words: Talking Spiritual Life, Living Spiritual Talk
6 x 9, 160 pp, Quality PB, 978-1-58023-020-9 **$16.95**

Eyes Remade for Wonder: A Lawrence Kushner Reader *Introduction by Thomas Moore*
6 x 9, 240 pp, Quality PB, 978-1-58023-042-1 **$18.95**

God Was in This Place & I, i Did Not Know: Finding Self, Spirituality and Ultimate
Meaning   6 x 9, 192 pp, Quality PB, 978-1-879045-33-0 **$16.95**

Honey from the Rock: An Introduction to Jewish Mysticism
6 x 9, 176 pp, Quality PB, 978-1-58023-073-5 **$16.95**

Invisible Lines of Connection: Sacred Stories of the Ordinary
5½ x 8½, 160 pp, Quality PB, 978-1-879045-98-9 **$15.95**

Jewish Spirituality—A Brief Introduction for Christians
5½ x 8½, 112 pp, Quality PB, 978-1-58023-150-3 **$12.95**

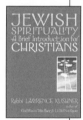

The River of Light: Jewish Mystical Awareness
6 x 9, 192 pp, Quality PB, 978-1-58023-096-4 **$16.95**

The Way Into Jewish Mystical Tradition
6 x 9, 224 pp, Quality PB, 978-1-58023-200-5 **$18.99**; HC, 978-1-58023-029-2 **$21.95**

Spirituality/Prayer

Pray Tell: A Hadassah Guide to Jewish Prayer
By Rabbi Jules Harlow, with contributions from many others
8½ x 11, 400 pp, Quality PB, 978-1-58023-163-3 **$29.95**

Witnesses to the One: The Spiritual History of the *Sh'ma* *By Rabbi Joseph B. Meszler;*
Foreword by Rabbi Elyse Goldstein 6 x 9, 176 pp, HC, 978-1-58023-309-5 **$19.99**

My People's Prayer Book Series

Traditional Prayers, Modern Commentaries   *Edited by Rabbi Lawrence A. Hoffman*
Provides diverse and exciting commentary to the traditional liturgy, helping modern
men and women find new wisdom in Jewish prayer, and bring liturgy into their lives.
Each book includes Hebrew text, modern translation, and commentaries from all
perspectives of the Jewish world.

Vol. 1—The *Sh'ma* and Its Blessings
7 x 10, 168 pp, HC, 978-1-879045-79-8 **$24.99**

Vol. 2—The *Amidah*
7 x 10, 240 pp, HC, 978-1-879045-80-4 **$24.95**

Vol. 3—*P'sukei D'zimrah* (Morning Psalms)
7 x 10, 240 pp, HC, 978-1-879045-81-1 **$24.95**

Vol. 4—*Seder K'riat Hatorah* (The Torah Service)
7 x 10, 264 pp, HC, 978-1-879045-82-8 **$23.95**

Vol. 5—*Birkhot Hashachar* (Morning Blessings)
7 x 10, 240 pp, HC, 978-1-879045-83-5 **$24.95**

Vol. 6—*Tachanun* and Concluding Prayers
7 x 10, 240 pp, HC, 978-1-879045-84-2 **$24.95**

Vol. 7—Shabbat at Home
7 x 10, 240 pp, HC, 978-1-879045-85-9 **$24.95**

Vol. 8—*Kabbalat Shabbat* (Welcoming Shabbat in the Synagogue)
7 x 10, 240 pp, HC, 978-1-58023-121-3 **$24.99**

Vol. 9—Welcoming the Night: *Minchah* and *Ma'ariv* (Afternoon and
Evening Prayer) 7 x 10, 272 pp, HC, 978-1-58023-262-3 **$24.99**

Vol. 10—Shabbat Morning: *Shacharit* and *Musaf* (Morning and Additional
Services) 7 x 10, 240 pp, HC, 978-1-58023-240-1 **$24.99**

Life Cycle
Marriage / Parenting / Family / Aging

Jewish Fathers: A Legacy of Love
Photographs by Lloyd Wolf. Essays by Paula Wolfson. Foreword by Rabbi Harold Kushner.
Honors the role of contemporary Jewish fathers in America. Each father tells in his own words what it means to be a parent and Jewish, and what he learned from his own father. Insightful photos.
10¾ x 9⅞, 144 pp with 100+ duotone photos, HC, 978-1-58023-204-3 **$30.00**

The New Jewish Baby Album: Creating and Celebrating the Beginning of a Spiritual Life—A Jewish Lights Companion
By the Editors at Jewish Lights. Foreword by Anita Diamant. Preface by Rabbi Sandy Eisenberg Sasso.
A spiritual keepsake that will be treasured for generations. More than just a memory book, *shows you how—and why it's important*—to create a Jewish home and a Jewish life. 8 x 10, 64 pp, Deluxe Padded HC, Full-color illus., 978-1-58023-138-1 **$19.95**

The Jewish Pregnancy Book: A Resource for the Soul, Body & Mind during Pregnancy, Birth & the First Three Months
By Sandy Falk, MD, and Rabbi Daniel Judson, with Steven A. Rapp
Includes medical information, prayers and rituals for each stage of pregnancy, from a liberal Jewish perspective. 7 x 10, 208 pp, Quality PB, b/w photos, 978-1-58023-178-7 **$16.95**

Celebrating Your New Jewish Daughter: Creating Jewish Ways to Welcome Baby Girls into the Covenant—New and Traditional Ceremonies *By Debra Nussbaum Cohen; Foreword by Rabbi Sandy Eisenberg Sasso* 6 x 9, 272 pp, Quality PB, 978-1-58023-090-2 **$18.95**

The New Jewish Baby Book, 2nd Edition: Names, Ceremonies & Customs—A Guide for Today's Families *By Anita Diamant* 6 x 9, 336 pp, Quality PB, 978-1-58023-251-7 **$19.99**

Parenting As a Spiritual Journey: Deepening Ordinary and Extraordinary Events into Sacred Occasions *By Rabbi Nancy Fuchs-Kreimer*
6 x 9, 224 pp, Quality PB, 978-1-58023-016-2 **$16.95**

Parenting Jewish Teens: A Guide for the Perplexed
By Joanne Doades 6 x 9, 200 pp, Quality PB, 978-1-58023-305-7 **$16.99**

Judaism for Two: A Spiritual Guide for Strengthening and Celebrating Your Loving Relationship *By Rabbi Nancy Fuchs-Kreimer and Rabbi Nancy H. Wiener; Foreword by Rabbi Elliot N. Dorff* Addresses the ways Jewish teachings can enhance and strengthen committed relationships. 6 x 9, 224 pp, Quality PB, 978-1-58023-254-8 **$16.99**

Embracing the Covenant: Converts to Judaism Talk About Why & How
By Rabbi Allan Berkowitz and Patti Moskovitz 6 x 9, 192 pp, Quality PB, 978-1-879045-50-7 **$16.95**

The Guide to Jewish Interfaith Family Life: An InterfaithFamily.com Handbook
Edited by Ronnie Friedland and Edmund Case 6 x 9, 384 pp, Quality PB, 978-1-58023-153-4 **$18.95**

Introducing My Faith and My Community
The Jewish Outreach Institute Guide for the Christian in a Jewish Interfaith Relationship
By Rabbi Kerry M. Olitzky 6 x 9, 176 pp, Quality PB, 978-1-58023-192-3 **$16.99**

Making a Successful Jewish Interfaith Marriage: The Jewish Outreach Institute Guide to Opportunities, Challenges and Resources *By Rabbi Kerry M. Olitzky with Joan Peterson Littman*
6 x 9, 176 pp, Quality PB, 978-1-58023-170-1 **$16.95**

The Creative Jewish Wedding Book: A Hands-On Guide to New & Old Traditions, Ceremonies & Celebrations *By Gabrielle Kaplan-Mayer*
9 x 9, 288 pp, b/w photos, Quality PB, 978-1-58023-194-7 **$19.99**

Divorce Is a Mitzvah: A Practical Guide to Finding Wholeness and Holiness When Your Marriage Dies *By Rabbi Perry Netter; Afterword by Rabbi Laura Geller.*
6 x 9, 224 pp, Quality PB, 978-1-58023-172-5 **$16.95**

A Heart of Wisdom: Making the Jewish Journey from Midlife through the Elder Years
Edited by Susan Berrin; Foreword by Harold Kushner
6 x 9, 384 pp, Quality PB, 978-1-58023-051-3 **$18.95**

So That Your Values Live On: Ethical Wills and How to Prepare Them
Edited by Jack Riemer and Nathaniel Stampfer
6 x 9, 272 pp, Quality PB, 978-1-879045-34-7 **$18.99**

Holidays/Holy Days

Rosh Hashanah Readings: Inspiration, Information and Contemplation
Yom Kippur Readings: Inspiration, Information and Contemplation
Edited by Rabbi Dov Peretz Elkins with Section Introductions from Arthur Green's These Are the Words
An extraordinary collection of readings, prayers and insights that enable the modern worshiper to enter into the spirit of the High Holy Days in a personal and powerful way, permitting the meaning of the Jewish New Year to enter the heart.
RHR: 6 x 9, 400 pp, HC, 978-1-58023-239-5 **$24.99**
YKR: 6 x 9, 368 pp, HC, 978-1-58023-271-5 **$24.99**

Jewish Holidays: A Brief Introduction for Christians
By Rabbi Kerry M. Olitzky and Rabbi Daniel Judson
5½ x 8½, 144 pp, Quality PB, 978-1-58023-302-6 **$16.99**

Leading the Passover Journey: The Seder's Meaning Revealed, the Haggadah's Story Retold *By Rabbi Nathan Laufer*
Uncovers the hidden meaning of the Seder's rituals and customs.
6 x 9, 224 pp, HC, 978-1-58023-211-1 **$24.99**

Reclaiming Judaism as a Spiritual Practice: Holy Days and Shabbat
By Rabbi Goldie Milgram
7 x 9, 272 pp, Quality PB, 978-1-58023-205-0 **$19.99**

7th Heaven: Celebrating Shabbat with Rebbe Nachman of Breslov
By Moshe Mykoff with the Breslov Research Institute
5⅛ x 8¼, 224 pp, Deluxe PB w/flaps, 978-1-58023-175-6 **$18.95**

The Women's Passover Companion: Women's Reflections on the Festival of Freedom *Edited by Rabbi Sharon Cohen Anisfeld, Tara Mohr, and Catherine Spector*
Groundbreaking. A provocative conversation about women's relationships to Passover as well as the roots and meanings of women's seders.
6 x 9, 352 pp, Quality PB, 978-1-58023-231-9 **$19.99**

The Women's Seder Sourcebook: Rituals & Readings for Use at the Passover Seder *Edited by Rabbi Sharon Cohen Anisfeld, Tara Mohr, and Catherine Spector*
Gathers the voices of more than one hundred women in readings, personal and creative reflections, commentaries, blessings, and ritual suggestions that can be incorporated into your Passover celebration.
6 x 9, 384 pp, Quality PB, 978-1-58023-232-6 **$19.99**

Creating Lively Passover Seders: A Sourcebook of Engaging Tales, Texts & Activities
By David Arnow, PhD 7 x 9, 416 pp, Quality PB, 978-1-58023-184-8 **$24.99**

Hanukkah, 2nd Edition: The Family Guide to Spiritual Celebration
By Dr. Ron Wolfson. Edited by Joel Lurie Grishaver.
7 x 9, 240 pp, illus., Quality PB, 978-1-58023-122-0 **$18.95**

The Jewish Family Fun Book: Holiday Projects, Everyday Activities, and Travel Ideas
with Jewish Themes *By Danielle Dardashti and Roni Sarig. Illus. by Avi Katz.*
6 x 9, 288 pp, 70+ b/w illus. & diagrams, Quality PB, 978-1-58023-171-8 **$18.95**

The Jewish Gardening Cookbook: Growing Plants & Cooking for Holidays
& Festivals *By Michael Brown* 6 x 9, 224 pp, 30+ b/w illus., Quality PB, 978-1-58023-116-9 **$16.95**

The Jewish Lights Book of Fun Classroom Activities: Simple and Seasonal
Projects for Teachers and Students *By Danielle Dardashti and Roni Sarig*
6 x 9, 240 pp, Quality PB, 978-1-58023-206-7 **$19.99**

Passover, 2nd Edition: The Family Guide to Spiritual Celebration
By Dr. Ron Wolfson with Joel Lurie Grishaver 7 x 9, 352 pp, Quality PB, 978-1-58023-174-9 **$19.95**

Shabbat, 2nd Edition: The Family Guide to Preparing for and Celebrating the Sabbath
By Dr. Ron Wolfson 7 x 9, 320 pp, illus., Quality PB, 978-1-58023-164-0 **$19.99**

Sharing Blessings: Children's Stories for Exploring the Spirit of the Jewish Holidays
By Rahel Musleah and Rabbi Michael Klayman
8½ x 11, 64 pp, Full-color illus., HC, 978-1-879045-71-2 **$18.95** *For ages 6 & up*

Inspiration

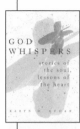

God's To-Do List: 103 Ways to Be an Angel and Do God's Work on Earth
By Dr. Ron Wolfson 6 x 9, 150 pp, Quality PB, 978-1-58023-301-9 **$15.99**

God in All Moments: Mystical & Practical Spiritual Wisdom from Hasidic Masters
Edited and translated by Or N. Rose with Ebn D. Leader
5½ x 8½, 192 pp, Quality PB, 978-1-58023-186-2 **$16.95**

Our Dance with God: Finding Prayer, Perspective and Meaning in the Stories of Our
Lives *By Karyn D. Kedar* 6 x 9, 176 pp, Quality PB, 978-1-58023-202-9 **$16.99**

Also Available: **The Dance of the Dolphin** (HC edition of *Our Dance with God*)
6 x 9, 176 pp, HC, 978-1-58023-154-1 **$19.95**

The Empty Chair: Finding Hope and Joy—Timeless Wisdom from a Hasidic Master,
Rebbe Nachman of Breslov *Adapted by Moshe Mykoff and the Breslov Research Institute*
4 x 6, 128 pp, 2-color text, Deluxe PB w/flaps, 978-1-879045-67-5 **$9.95**

The Gentle Weapon: Prayers for Everyday and Not-So-Everyday Moments—
Timeless Wisdom from the Teachings of the Hasidic Master, Rebbe Nachman of Breslov
Adapted by Moshe Mykoff and S. C. Mizrahi, together with the Breslov Research Institute
4 x 6, 144 pp, 2-color text, Deluxe PB w/flaps, 978-1-58023-022-3 **$9.99**

God Whispers: Stories of the Soul, Lessons of the Heart *By Karyn D. Kedar*
6 x 9, 176 pp, Quality PB, 978-1-58023-088-9 **$15.95**

An Orphan in History: One Man's Triumphant Search for His Jewish Roots
By Paul Cowan; Afterword by Rachel Cowan. 6 x 9, 288 pp, Quality PB, 978-1-58023-135-0 **$16.95**

Restful Reflections: Nighttime Inspiration to Calm the Soul, Based on Jewish Wisdom
By Rabbi Kerry M. Olitzky & Rabbi Lori Forman 4½ x 6½, 448 pp, Quality PB, 978-1-58023-091-9 **$15.95**

Sacred Intentions: Daily Inspiration to Strengthen the Spirit, Based on Jewish Wisdom
By Rabbi Kerry M. Olitzky and Rabbi Lori Forman 4½ x 6½, 448 pp, Quality PB, 978-1-58023-061-2 **$15.95**

Kabbalah/Mysticism/Enneagram

Awakening to Kabbalah: The Guiding Light of Spiritual Fulfillment
By Rav Michael Laitman, PhD 6 x 9, 192 pp, HC, 978-1-58023-264-7 **$21.99**

Seek My Face: A Jewish Mystical Theology *By Arthur Green*
6 x 9, 304 pp, Quality PB, 978-1-58023-130-5 **$19.95**

Zohar: Annotated & Explained
Translation and annotation by Daniel C. Matt; Foreword by Andrew Harvey
5½ x 8½, 176 pp, Quality PB, 978-1-893361-51-5 **$15.99** *(A SkyLight Paths book)*

Cast in God's Image: Discover Your Personality Type Using the Enneagram and Kabbalah
By Rabbi Howard A. Addison
7 x 9, 176 pp, Quality PB, Layflat binding, 20+ journaling exercises, 978-1-58023-124-4 **$16.95**

Ehyeh: A Kabbalah for Tomorrow
By Arthur Green 6 x 9, 224 pp, Quality PB, 978-1-58023-213-5 **$16.99**

The Enneagram and Kabbalah, 2nd Edition: Reading Your Soul
By Rabbi Howard A. Addison 6 x 9, 192 pp, Quality PB, 978-1-58023-229-6 **$16.99**

Finding Joy: A Practical Spiritual Guide to Happiness *By Dannel I. Schwartz with Mark Hass*
6 x 9, 192 pp, Quality PB, 978-1-58023-009-4 **$14.95**

The Flame of the Heart: Prayers of a Chasidic Mystic *By Reb Noson of Breslov. Translated by
David Sears with the Breslov Research Institute* 5 x 7¼, 160 pp, Quality PB, 978-1-58023-246-3 **$15.99**

The Gift of Kabbalah: Discovering the Secrets of Heaven, Renewing Your Life on Earth
By Tamar Frankiel, PhD 6 x 9, 256 pp, Quality PB, 978-1-58023-141-1 **$16.95;**
HC, 978-1-58023-108-4 **$21.95**

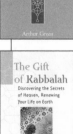

Kabbalah: A Brief Introduction for Christians
By Tamar Frankiel, PhD 5½ x 8½, 208 pp, Quality PB, 978-1-58023-303-3 **$16.99**

The Lost Princess and Other Kabbalistic Tales of Rebbe Nachman of Breslov
The Seven Beggars and Other Kabbalistic Tales of Rebbe Nachman of Breslov
Translated by Rabbi Aryeh Kaplan; Preface by Rabbi Chaim Kramer
Lost Princess: 6 x 9, 400 pp, Quality PB, 978-1-58023-217-3 **$18.99**
Seven Beggars: 6 x 9, 192 pp, Quality PB, 978-1-58023-250-0 **$16.99**

See also *The Way Into Jewish Mystical Tradition* in Spirituality / The Way Into... Series

Spirituality/Women's Interest

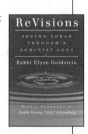

The Quotable Jewish Woman: Wisdom, Inspiration & Humor from the Mind & Heart
Edited and compiled by Elaine Bernstein Partnow
6 x 9, 496 pp, HC, 978-1-58023-193-0 **$29.99**

The Knitting Way: A Guide to Spiritual Self-Discovery *By Linda Skolnick and Janice MacDaniels* 7 x 9, 240 pp, Quality PB, 978-1-59473-079-5 **$16.99** *(A SkyLight Paths book)*

The Quilting Path: A Guide to Spiritual Self-Discovery through Fabric, Thread and Kabbalah
By Louise Silk 7 x 9, 192 pp, Quality PB, 978-1-59473-206-5 **$16.99** *(A SkyLight Paths book)*

The Divine Feminine in Biblical Wisdom Literature: Selections Annotated &
Explained *Translated and Annotated by Rabbi Rami Shapiro*
5½ x 8½, 240 pp, Quality PB, 978-1-59473-109-9 **$16.99** *(A SkyLight Paths book)*

Lifecycles, Vol. 1: Jewish Women on Life Passages & Personal Milestones
Edited and with Introductions by Rabbi Debra Orenstein
6 x 9, 480 pp, Quality PB, 978-1-58023-018-6 **$19.95**

Lifecycles, Vol. 2: Jewish Women on Biblical Themes in Contemporary Life
Edited and with Introductions by Rabbi Debra Orenstein and Rabbi Jane Rachel Litman
6 x 9, 464 pp, Quality PB, 978-1-58023-019-3 **$19.95**

Moonbeams: A Hadassah Rosh Hodesh Guide *Edited by Carol Diament, PhD*
8½ x 11, 240 pp, Quality PB, 978-1-58023-099-5 **$20.00**

ReVisions: Seeing Torah through a Feminist Lens *By Rabbi Elyse Goldstein*
5½ x 8½, 224 pp, Quality PB, 978-1-58023-117-6 **$16.95**

The Women's Haftarah Commentary: New Insights from Women Rabbis on the
54 Weekly Haftarah Portions, the 5 Megillot & Special Shabbatot
Edited by Rabbi Elyse Goldstein 6 x 9, 560 pp, HC, 978-1-58023-133-6 **$39.99**

The Women's Torah Commentary: New Insights from Women Rabbis on the 54
Weekly Torah Portions *Edited by Rabbi Elyse Goldstein*
6 x 9, 496 pp, HC, 978-1-58023-076-6 **$34.95**

The Year Mom Got Religion: One Woman's Midlife Journey into Judaism
By Lee Meyerhoff Hendler 6 x 9, 208 pp, Quality PB, 978-1-58023-070-4 **$15.95**

See Holidays for *The Women's Passover Companion: Women's Reflections on the Festival of Freedom* and *The Women's Seder Sourcebook: Rituals & Readings for Use at the Passover Seder.* Also see Bar/Bat Mitzvah for *The JGirl's Guide: The Young Jewish Woman's Handbook for Coming of Age.*

Travel

Israel—A Spiritual Travel Guide, 2nd Edition
A Companion for the Modern Jewish Pilgrim
By Rabbi Lawrence A. Hoffman 4¾ x 10, 256 pp, Quality PB, illus., 978-1-58023-261-6 **$18.99**
Also Available: **The Israel Mission Leader's Guide** 978-1-58023-085-8 **$4.95**

12-Step

100 Blessings Every Day: Daily Twelve Step Recovery Affirmations, Exercises for
Personal Growth & Renewal Reflecting Seasons of the Jewish Year
By Rabbi Kerry M. Olitzky; Foreword by Rabbi Neil Gillman
4½ x 6½, 432 pp, Quality PB, 978-1-879045-30-9 **$15.99**

Recovery from Codependence: A Jewish Twelve Steps Guide to Healing Your Soul
By Rabbi Kerry M. Olitzky 6 x 9, 160 pp, Quality PB, 978-1-879045-32-3 **$13.95**

Renewed Each Day: Daily Twelve Step Recovery Meditations Based on the Bible
By Rabbi Kerry M. Olitzky and Aaron Z.
Vol. 1—Genesis & Exodus: 6 x 9, 224 pp, Quality PB, 978-1-879045-12-5 **$14.95**
Vol. 2—Leviticus, Numbers & Deuteronomy: 6 x 9, 280 pp, Quality PB, 978-1-879045-13-2 **$18.99**

Twelve Jewish Steps to Recovery: A Personal Guide to Turning from Alcoholism &
Other Addictions—Drugs, Food, Gambling, Sex ...
By Rabbi Kerry M. Olitzky and Stuart A. Copans, MD; Preface by Abraham J. Twerski, MD
6 x 9, 144 pp, Quality PB, 978-1-879045-09-5 **$14.95**

About Jewish Lights

People of all faiths and backgrounds yearn for books that attract, engage, educate, and spiritually inspire.

Our principal goal is to stimulate thought and help all people learn about who the Jewish People are, where they come from, and what the future can be made to hold. While people of our diverse Jewish heritage are the primary audience, our books speak to people in the Christian world as well and will broaden their understanding of Judaism and the roots of their own faith.

We bring to you authors who are at the forefront of spiritual thought and experience. While each has something different to say, they all say it in a voice that you can hear.

Our books are designed to welcome you and then to engage, stimulate, and inspire. We judge our success not only by whether or not our books are beautiful and commercially successful, but by whether or not they make a difference in your life.

For your information and convenience, at the back of this book we have provided a list of other Jewish Lights books you might find interesting and useful. They cover all the categories of your life:

Bar/Bat Mitzvah
Bible Study / Midrash
Children's Books
Congregation Resources
Current Events / History
Ecology
Fiction: Mystery, Science Fiction
Grief / Healing
Holidays / Holy Days
Inspiration
Kabbalah / Mysticism / Enneagram

Life Cycle
Meditation
Parenting
Prayer
Ritual / Sacred Practice
Spirituality
Theology / Philosophy
Travel
12-Step
Women's Interest

Stuart M. Matlins, Publisher

Or phone, fax, mail or e-mail to: **JEWISH LIGHTS Publishing**
Sunset Farm Offices, Route 4 • P.O. Box 237 • Woodstock, Vermont 05091
Tel: (802) 457-4000 • Fax: (802) 457-4004 • www.jewishlights.com
Credit card orders: (800) 962-4544 (8:30AM–5:30PM ET Monday–Friday)
Generous discounts on quantity orders. SATISFACTION GUARANTEED. Prices subject to change.

**For more information about each book,
visit our website at www.jewishlights.com**